The Prime Minister

For David Lampos

The Prime Minister

with love

AUSTIN CLARKE

Austin Clarke

5 Dec 94

Exile Editions
TORONTO

1994

•

This Edition is published by Exile Editions Limited,
20 Dale Avenue, Toronto, Ontario, Canada M4W 1K4

Sales Distribution
General Publishing Co. Ltd.,
30 Lesmill Road, Don Mills, Ontario M3B 2T6

•

Design by ALLAN SANDERS
Typeset by MOONS OF JUPITER
Printed by BEST BOOK MANUFACTURERS
Cover by ALLAN SANDERS
Author's photograph by ROB ALLEN

The author wishes to thank
the Ontario Arts Council for its support.

The publisher wishes to acknowledge
the assistance towards publication
of the Canada Council, the Ontario Arts Council,
and the Ministry of Culture, Tourism, & Recreation.

ISBN 1-55096-0660

TO MURIEL SEALY
Black, blessed and beautiful Woman

The land is beautiful. When you come in upon it from the low height of a plane, it looks like a fairyland. The local officials who advertise it in brochures and in countries overseas refer to it as paradise. The tourists say it really is paradise. Everything in this paradise is cheap, they boast. "The native women are cheap, the native help is cheap, and it is the best super vacation in the world."

In the crowded hilarious plane of tourists coming for their seven days of paradise, everyone became tense, especially the tourists, and from the windows they saw that the land looked beautiful. There was a bullet of light smashing through the valley of various shades of green; and the hills were laughing as the tourists were now laughing at their new-found paradise. A Canadian man sitting beside his wife exclaimed, "For two hundred and ten bucks! That is *all* it costs! What a deal, what a super deal!"

Beside the Canadian, on the aisle seat, was the lone native man in that row of roaring tourists. He searched inside his breast pocket for the Air Canada ticket, to see what his return flight from Toronto had cost him. He pulled out instead a letter written to him in Toronto by a minister of government. This letter was the cause of his being on this flight. He was going home after twenty years, to take up a job with the government. The letter had said "Private & Confidential;" and it was a long letter. He had read the letter seven times; and had underlined two sections of it which he considered were the most important: " . . . *that we disestablish the post of Chief Information Officer and create a non-civil service contract post of Director of Cultural Relations, Director of National Culture*

and Information Services, or whatever title is decided upon."
And this more ironical section: *"This would be the kind of job which would last only the life of a government."*

He did not realize until he had the letter in his hand now how tentative the job was. His closest friend had said that, he remembered now. They had been drinking at the Park Plaza roof bar, which had been their hangout for fifteen years. He had said something about patriotism; and his friend, who was a successful lawyer, had laughed. His friend always laughed whenever he talked about patriotism. The clouds above the hotel had been grey that afternoon. He was seeing those same clouds now, as the plane was pushing through the valley of the beautiful land he was coming home to; with the tourists who called it paradise.

"... regulations require that we spray this plane with..."

He had traveled to a few cities in Canada and in the northern United States, at the height of his career as a poet; and never once had he seen a stewardess spraying a plane before landing. It could be that in the tropics, which had a peculiar smell, this was the new custom. He had been away too long. He tried to guess the scent the stewardess would use. But she came down the aisle like a purge, squirting an unknown scent over the heads of the Canadian tourists and the few West Indians, tired from the long flight.

He started to sneeze. His sinus troubles were returning. Not since he had left this land, twenty years ago, had he suffered from sinus. He was returning home.

"Where's the easiest place to find women? Where can we get some cheap native women?"

He was looking through the window on the other side of the aisle, the only view of his home that was possible and convenient to him in the crowded tourist plane.

What had this flight cost him? He must find the Air Canada ticket folder. But the tourist asked the question again; and this time he could not mistake, nor pretend that his knowledge of the land and of the women in this paradise was not being propositioned. "Hey, friend! How do we find the broads on this island? Maybe you could fix us up yourself, eh?" The tourist was speaking to him. Could it be a simple case of a stranger seeking directions? But he had never, in twenty years, asked a Torontonian about "broads." It might have been the cultural difference between them. Some people went to the bathroom on the street, others in a closet.

He tried to remember the land. This was a land where people acted. He remembered that much about the land. It was true that in some cases, which he had read about in Toronto, they had acted badly. These acts were surrounded by a lack of wisdom, by indecency and corruption. That was politics. Everybody said politics was like that. But he was not a politician. He was a poet. Still, the problem bothered him. Had the people who had to live in this paradise really stopped thinking, simply because the land was a paradise?

He then remembered, for what reason he didn't know, that when he was at the college at home, his favorite poem had been "Paradise Lost." He had liked "Paradise Regained," too; but the English master, who was an Englishman, never spent much time on "Paradise Regained." And the master never did tell his class of predominantly lower-class native black children whether he himself preferred "Paradise Lost." He had promised then, even before he ever thought of becoming a poet, indeed he had vowed then, that when he had time, in later years, he would really make a study of "Paradise Regained" to see whether there was any insinuation in the English master's lack of emphasis on it. But the plane was now rushing through the narrow end of the valley with the explosion of fading afternoon and light. He looked at his country going past his view, like the frames in a magic lantern, shown at too fast a speed for concentration and identification. And so he gave in to the circumstance of arrival, with the loud expectations of glee and greed; and with the man from Canada asking him how cheap "his women" were; and with no concrete thoughts about his return, he settled back to witness and feel again, after twenty years, how beautiful the land was; and the feel of love and loving in the eyes of the women he had remembered, black in their resisted African beauty, preferring to see themselves as women of various American and Canadian models. But they were themselves beautiful. And the beauty of his black blessed women made him feel starved from all those years in Canada. Some of these women would now be at the crowded pushing rails on the roof of the arrivals room; and more of them would be on tiptoe, or suspended for the moment of a glance of recognition, jumping up for more height, to see who was coming in on this plane. The women would be there. And the man from Canada could watch them in this new moment of history, when the price for one of them might be even cheaper than it had been in the village in the valley years ago, when the sun shot through like a memory.

What was the fragrance of the spray they used to cleanse the plane with, just before they left the pure heights of clouds and whisky and cigars from Cuba legal in the air? Was it the smell of Lysol? The plane was circling, ruminating over the land for the correct spot on which to land. Twenty years ago, his grandmother, who was the best pharmacist in the island in the practice of herbs which she grew around the inside paling of her small backyard of her small house, and "bush-teas" which she made from miraculous bush and sersey and other bushes handed down to her from some place in Africa, and now buried in the unworked ground as they were in his memory; this ancient woman, too experienced to be called simply old, with the lines of history running up and down her face, washed the "life-sore" on a neighbor's child's left shin, unhealed like an open cancer for five years, with Lysol. Lysol was, to him, a liquid of purity and poverty and of healing. Perhaps it was that; perhaps it was for that reason that the stewardess had sprayed the plane with a fragrance which smelled like Lysol. He wished they would tell you more things on planes. He wished there were people like his grandmother. There would be at least one woman like his grandmother waiting for this plane to arrive. And lots of other people, mostly women, waiting to honor someone's arrival; to greet him early, and to get to him before any more distant relations could get to him, to demand shares in the gifts that were always brought from Away. He had heard before he left Toronto that the unemployment here was more than thirty percent. When he was still living in the land, he would see young men and women and older women and older men "with nothing to do" pass on the long only road to this same airport to see a plane come in. In those days, to see a plane come in was like going to a movie. And on their return, slow like an excursion bus tottering home in exhaustion and some drunkenness, they would stop and tell you "who come in" and "who was leffing;" and if they had time left, if they were not going to church — for those visits to the airport were made usually on Sunday afternoons — they would tell you what their philosophy on departure and emigration was. Some would tell you that it was better to leave this place than to remain in it "and dead" from having nothing to do. And then they would talk about the unemployment in the island, although they never called it "unemployment," certainly not by that name. And they never measured their participation in having nothing to do by percentages. But they would tell you, "If it wasn't for that sister o' mine living in the States, I don't know what the hell I would do." And they would all agree, and move farther down the slow road, and perhaps think of going to church after all, for there was nothing to do.

All this went through his mind as the large plane rushed through the last small green fields in the valley approaching the runway. And the feeling of arriving, of landing, filled his body and he was overjoyed; and was almost certain now that he had made the best decision by returning home. The second portion in the minister's letter came clearly before him: *This would be the kind of job which would last only the life of a government.* He was home now. He had called his mother in New York, where she had emigrated years ago, to tell her; and his mother had told him, "What are you retrograding now for, boy?" He had no answer for his mother. "Well," she had said, closing the conversation, "home is home." The land surrounding him came to a full stop. Then there was a more stable viewing of the slides of people through the frames of the windows. The plane was crawling into the parking area. The tourists were moving about the plane. Some seemed to have already forgotten the winter coats which out of habit they had brought along with them; and all had expressions of joy and anticipation on their faces. They were like people transformed. The door of the plane opened, and there was an explosion of white bodies on the runway.

When he stepped down from the last shaking rung, he felt like kissing the ground. But there was a difference between kissing a runway and kissing a piece of land, black and moldy and waiting for the plough; and there might be someone waiting, someone who might have remembered that he was a poet, and who might miscalculate the gesture, and brand him as a radical, or something like that. He had to be careful about returning home after all these years. His instincts told him that. And all of a sudden he did not feel free to do it. He was home.

The large crowd moved into the waiting room where the black policemen, immigration officers, were; and he looked around him again, and except for the policemen in the vast room, and the anxious Red Caps waiting to pounce upon the baggage in the adjoining glassed-off room, he did not know that he was in his native land. He was surrounded by Canadians. There were five other black persons in the lines with him. He would never know what they were thinking of this arrival.

Someone came from inside where the Red Caps were pressed flat to the face against the glass wall, gesturing to the tourists to do business with them; and the anxious tourists, understanding the custom, promised them their business, with nods and other movements of the body, because their hands were filled with boxes of duty-free Canadian Club. Some of the gestures the

Canadians made to the Red Caps meant other things in Toronto. But everybody was saying how the land was progressing and becoming North American in habit and in wealth.

He could not breathe as he stood at the end of his line. The air was oppressive and his seersucker suit was sticking to his body. The Red Caps were rushing for luggage.

He was now in front of an immigration policeman. He relaxed, feeling pride in being examined by one of his countrymen. He had never seen a black immigration officer anywhere at any of the airports where he had traveled. He handed his documents to the policeman. He was more relaxed now. The policeman's short-sleeved white tunic was soiled under the arms. He too must be suffering from the humidity in the room which did not have air conditioning.

"Passport, please."

He was thinking of asking the immigration officer how he felt living in a "new" country; but he changed his mind, and gave him the passport. Years ago he had thought of applying for a Canadian passport; but he had decided against it. His country had become independent while he had been away from it; and he wanted to boast in celebration of this independence by carrying his country's passport. He felt very proud handing his country's independent passport to one of his country's own black immigration policemen.

"How long you staying?"

The policeman did not recognize him as one of his countrymen; perhaps there was the mark of the foreigner on him, on his clothes, on his enthusiasm about the new country and about independence, which the policeman could not differentiate from former times.

An enraged Canadian writing in the newspapers about the sudden increase of West Indian immigrants to

Canada had asked in a letter to the editor: *"Why if they do not like it here, and do not seem to be able to get along with us, don't they go back to the jungles where they come from?"*

"You hear what I ask you? How long are you staying?"

"I was born here, man!"

"Who are you calling 'man?' Address me as 'Sir.' Now how long?"

"I was born in this country."

The immigration policeman turned the pages of the passport, looking for something, apparently finding it, and then changing his expression of belligerence slightly, said, "I could have sworn you looked like one o' them North American radicals! Anyhow ... "

He passed through the narrow door in the glassed-off wall, and went to look for his bags. He took the three of them to the customs officer, who seemed to have been stationed there to inspect him personally. Most of the tourists had been examined by the immigration officers with no questions asked; and had been waved through by the customs officers. He could not understand the preferential treatment they were reserving for him.

"Open. Open up," the young brown-skinned customs officer said. He was dressed like a junior officer in a navy, perhaps a Royal Navy. "All o' them! Open-up all three o' them!"

"Yes, sir," he said. The customs officer did not smile.

He flung back the unzipped tops of the three bags, and the officer fumbled his short stubby fingers through the shirts and the ties and the underwear, with no regard to the silken delicacy of the owner's underwear. He looked like a man with his long hand into a crab hole searching for a crab which he was going to eat, and meant to eat, because he was sure he would find something. As he searched, he looked up at the bewildered man standing in front of him; and he added just a little more officialdom to his young face, intent upon making the new arrival understand the seriousness of arriving in the young, new, independent country. In the second unzipped bag, the officer found some copies of a volume of poems. He took them all up, and then put back all except one, which he examined. He read the biographical notes on the back jacket cover, carefully checked the likeness of photograph against examinee, slapped the book shut, and then took up the copy of *Viva* magazine. His face muscles flinched slightly as his eyes rested on the nude women in the magazine, and then he put the magazine down. He leafed through the copy of *The Wretched Of The Earth*, his hands seeming to tremble as he passed his eyes over some random lines in the chapter on revolution; and in this manner of controlled anxiety, he beckoned to the unoccupied other customs officer behind him to come and see. Together they looked at the section of the book, eccentric in their facial expressions, the exchange of which meant nothing at all to him, and then they moved away. He remained waiting to see what they would do. There was no one else in the baggage section. The tourists had all left. And he was alone. After a long time, time in which he would get some indication of the psychological picture they were trying to paint and imprint upon his mind, the first customs officer said, without coming back to him, "We're finished with you."

He took his three bags, one by one, outside. The loading area was empty. The air was stifling and choking, and the humidity was like an armor of lead lining his seersucker suit. He could have been in Canada, in the bone-chilling winter, where one night he was made to remain in the immigration section at the airport in Toronto for two hours while some slight problem about his entry from the United States was being contested. Here, in the heat of arriving, he was not really at home. All the taxis had left with the tourists and only a few men who worked at the airport were moving about aimlessly and slowly, as if they had agreed to give the heat its due. The loading area showed the evidence of a large crowd which had recently left: a page from a newspaper taken up in the wind swirled around twice and then gallivanted down into the parking lot, in the direction of the valley through which the plane had entered, distant and half asleep in the afternoon of siesta'ed disregard. The page of newspaper came silently back up towards him, like a dislocated airplane wing, and landed just below his feet. He looked down, and full in the middle of the page was his photograph, taken twenty years ago. "POET RETURNS AFTER TWO DECADES TO HEAD LOCAL CULTURE." Tires and recent footprints had left their mark on the entire story that went with the photograph; so he could not read what they had said about his returning. He was home. And he was alone.

"One thing about this place, boy. Be careful of what you talk. It's not the same place you left twenty years ago. This place changed. I don't know if for the good, or . . . " The waiter moved in front of them with a tray of drinks: rum and ginger, rum and soda, scotch and soda and scotch and water. He took a scotch and water, while his friend took what looked like scotch and soda. The waiter looked long at him, smiled, and said, "You come back." It was spoken as a question; and at the same time it sounded like a statement. His time away from the language was causing him great discomfort in following the speech, and there were nuances in the speech which he could not grasp. He had thought of the immigration policeman's comment, *"How long are you staying?"* all the way down in the taxi, which had arrived just before he had given up hope. The language in its frequency of usage, in its native context, now put itself up against him; and it emphasized him as a stranger in his own country. "As I was telling you, old man. The changes that have taken place in this place, well, sometimes I myself feel like an expatriate, you know what I mean? Well, like a touriss, then."

"I saw some houses that were the same twenty years ago."

"They build some new ones though."

"Some of the things I see are the same."

"Well, the same and not the same."

"A customs-fellow gave me a hard time at the airport, this afternoon."

"A customs-fellow . . . " He was thinking of something. Then he said, "Do you mean a brown-skin fellow with good hair, what we call 'good-hair?' And two stripes on his shoulder?"

"That is him, man!"

"He's a member of the Other party, the opposition party," his friend told him. "You see, you were in the papers for the last three or so days. And that brown-skin fellow is a cousin of the man who is your deputy." He went on to talk more about the cousin and the job, and how important a job it was to some people.

"What is it really like?"

"Read the *Weekly*. You would never know you're living in the same country."

"The new newspaper?"

"It running this blasted country now, boy."

"Does the government own it?"

"The *Weekly*, or the country?"

"Who controls it?"

"Foreign money. From up North where you come from."

His friend took a long sip of his drink, contemplating his answer, and he rolled his eyes, as he had been in the habit of doing for years now; this much idiosyncrasy hadn't changed. His friend took this long sip and rolled his eyes around half the arc of serious conversation that required a serious answer; and the answer had to give the impression that it was born of preparation in thought. If you did not understand that, you did not understand the rolling of the eyes and the long contemplative sip. He understood, in his present state of undercomprehension of statements, many of which he was mistaking for questions, and his unease with nuance, that the statement to follow the rolling of eyes could very well be the one statement which would open the shell of mystery which seemed to lock these people in self-assuring arrogance from the superficial inquiring glance. Or it might be, quite simply, their inability to be candid. He had stayed away too long to see whether, in fact, there was any substance contained in the statement.

He was not really being engaged in conversation; he was standing before a fairly well-placed comfortable man, who did not have the time nor the disposition for the give-and-take of conversation, but who, because of his position and because of the new significance given to that position in a country recently independent, was a man who made only statements. Statements of power. Lesser men would have to follow; and pick the main clause from the complication and the string of other clauses. The man was rolling his eyes again: time to listen and concentrate. He must listen carefully for that single statement embedded in the sentence which would contain the solution.

"I told you a moment ago, the *Weekly* run this place, *literally*." There was slight chance to make a conversation out of these pronouncements. At any rate, he would have to know about the real power in the country; and who owned it. He had heard already, in the short time since he had returned, that the most powerful person in the country was a woman. And he wondered why. His friend described this woman as having grey eyes, resembling a cat's, and a body that had grown tired and old through use, and a disease which everybody knew about, cancer; and that it was just a matter of time before she surrendered to the cancer. This woman, he said, had a lot of power, a lot of power. One man who said he knew her since she was a girl, forty years ago, said that she got this power from the first time she "dropped her drawers." He said that all this great power she had was "right there, right down there. Down there so." He had touched his trousers fly. "That's where she have this great source o' power."

His friend was still talking, and rolling his eyes. That was another thing. He must learn to be more attentive. He could not concentrate long enough to understand the meaning behind words; and the words were often spoken in a different accent, so that most of the time was taken up in following the accent. "If you want to know what's going on in this country, and if you want to know what should be going on, all you have to do is read the *Weekly*. For instance, last year the *Weekly* wrote an article on one-party state, and you see, the government got thirty-two seats out of forty in the House, and although the government never really officially came out and said in plain language that it wanted a one-party state, would you believe that that article the *Weekly* published had the government apologizing about wanting a one-party state? As a matter of fact, certain people in this community believe . . . between me and you . . . that the government had secret plans to turn the place into a dictatorship, or a republic."

They were at a cocktail party. It was being held in one of the better residential developments. Everything these days was development. It was the new word for a new road built in a place previously overrun with bushes. Here the houses were all constructed on the same architectural pattern, with spacious lawns, most of which were planted in zinnias, chalice vines, and the flaming red oleander. On this lawn there were about fifty persons, young men and women mainly, who, judging from the way they were dressed and the assured manner in which they held their drinks, swirling the glass round and round and turning the ice cubes into dull tongs of bells, were obviously from the upper middle class. He tried to compare this party with those he knew in Toronto. All these women wore long dresses. The patterns in the dresses were like the resplendent colors of the tropics. Not one woman wore a dress that did not have at least three colors in it. The men were all in the "shirtjack" suit, the official attire of the newly independent country. He was in a new world. A black maid dressed in starchy white, with a white serving cap on her

Afro hairdo, mingled in with the guests serving drinks. And before you had time to drink half your drink, one of the three black butlers in white shirt and black trousers and black tie was handing you another. You could not tell, standing here, in this cool tropical late afternoon, that thirty percent of the population was unemployed; there was no reminder of the high cost of living which everybody was talking about, and of the high cost of food and imported scotch which everybody was drinking. His friend said that the Other party was going to take over the country; and that they should take over. The atmosphere was tense, even as he saw his country in this short time. The high cost of living and the rate of inflation had affected everything: "Even the wages I have to pay my maid, darling." But they had apparently not affected this group of people, merry with drink and happy, with the sea down the blue hill, and the breeze in the oleanders and the mayflower tree.

"Johnmoore!"

The voice came from the other side of the lawn. It was a loud voice. A carefree voice.

"Jesus Christ! Look who's in the land! When you come back, man?"

The greeting had the effect of keeping him breathless and unmoving, until he recognized the man. He had never heard his name called out like that, as one word, like a common noun. And it was the first time since his return that anyone had called his name.

"Johnmoore!" the man said again, joining Christian name to surname. It was like an identification mark, his own identification mark; and at the same time, it was a gesture of recognition and acceptance. "Johnmoore, man, how long have you been back?"

"Yesterday," he said, confused by the oppression of time and strange faces. "No! A few hours ago." And in this state, he tried to place the face in history and time.

Each face he had seen since his return, each hand he had shaken, had to be carefully placed in time over many years.

"Well, Jesus Christ! Up there really agreed with you. Man, you even looking more younger than when you left."

"The cold weather."

"How many years now?"

"Winter, man!"

"Congrats, though. We need people like you. People who been abroad and who decide to come back and help. Even if you are a radical poet as the papers said. Congratulations."

"Johnmoore, let me introduce you to ... "

"You introducing me to Johnmoore?" Johnmoore did not know the newcomer's name; and he could not remember his friend's name. No one introduced himself by name; they were sure that name and face had been carried by Johnmoore intact over all that vastness of disjointed time and place. "Weekesie," the newcomer said, "me and Johnmoore grow-up in poverty together. He was bound to be a poet. Not like you, you bastard. You're in the touriss-business now. Corning money offa the tourisses."

"Johnmoore was just telling me," Weekesie said, trying to be neutral, "that a lot o' them came in on his plane. The place overrun."

"Pussy like peas in town tonight!" the newcomer said, crudely. There appeared to be some secrets and some rivalry between these two men.

"How do you feel with all these strangers among you?" Johnmoore asked. "Don't you feel strange?" Neither of them made a comment. Perhaps it was the wrong kind of question to ask so soon. But he wanted to find out. People in this part of the world did not look on tourism the same way as those who lived abroad. These local men were making him uneasy. They seemed to be so contented, and so broadminded. "Tourists are not good for the development of a free country," he said.

"You are just a blasted radical, boy!" the newcomer said.

"Tourism is *we*, boy," Weekesie said. He wanted to avert the argument.

"You got to realize something, fast, boy," the newcomer said. There was viciousness in his tone. "You think you could just come here and make statements to take dollar-bills outta people's hands. How could you come from whereverthehell you was in North America, and make a statement like 'Tourism not good for a developing country?' You don't even live here!"

He must remember to be careful not to apply his North American perspective to things which belonged to the island.

"All this that you see here," Weekesie said, pointing to the well-groomed lawn, and to the splendid flowers and the people in comfortable knots of gossip and light talk, "All this, tourism brought to this country."

"A Canadian fellow on the plane asked me to help him find some cheap native women."

"What kind o' women?" Weekesie asked.

"Native women."

"He actually said *native women?*"

"There ain't nothing wrong with that, man!" the newcomer said. He put an end to any further argument by the secure matter-of-fact way he spoke. That was another thing that he would have to learn: the way people here could end the most serious conversation or discussion by such a small, stupid rejoinder. But it was the arrogance in the man's rejoinder that worried him. He detected some trace of power in the usage of the words.

He was getting tired.

"Imagine. I told you I came in yesterday, when in fact I arrived only . . . "

"I know you didn' come yesterday. One o' the police in the immigration called me the moment you passed through," the newcomer said.

The long trip and the large number of drinks he had had since arriving were wearing him down. He had had no time to eat; and the delicacies which were being served at this cocktail party made his appetite more ravenous. He must remember to inquire about a good place to have a meal. The newcomer seemed to have read his thoughts, and said, "I would suggest a place to eat, but even as a man who makes a small living offa these blasted tourisses, the best places to have a bite is where the tourisses does eat. And you would understand that that kind o' food wasn't intended for me and you."

"Yeah, all the best places is touriss places," Weekesie said.

But he was more interested in the land. The land had remained unspoiled in spite of the trampled gutting it had been subjected to; and all around him he could see the land. It had undergone an invasion from the North; and even though the occupation was but for seven or fourteen days' duration at a time, the impact, it seemed, had already been indelible. The native people were now serving the tourists. And the native people were now serving canned peaches of the worst brand, from abroad; and had stopped eating their own local fruits, such as sugar apple, pawpaw, and mango, Weekesie said. Things were really changing, he said. But he seemed to relish the change because it brought great wealth with it.

"The common-man still catching his arse, though," the newcomer said. "And not one o' them would talk 'bout it. People don't talk about those things no more. Nowadays, everybody frightened. Everybody feel that the government ain't no blasted good, but they won't tell you so. People don't talk freely anymore. And still, only last month, in an American magazine, this country was voted the freest country in the whole world! The freest country in the whole world!"

"Which American magazine?" he asked the newcomer.

But without answering, the newcomer left to talk to some woman.

"Oh, look! I want you to meet that man over there, with the dog collar. The Reverend."

They moved along beside small groups of men and women. He could not make out the gist of conversations; they were moving too fast for that, and the language was still new to him. He had been home for only six or seven hours. He wondered whether he would ever learn the language again, to speak it with its characteristic deceit and hypocrisy, the way he listened to Weekesie and the newcomer use it. It was not that he thought Weekesie was deceitful and a hypocrite; it was merely his use of the language. They were now beside a woman with a flushed round face, who was speaking with a very tall man who wore a white beard trimmed like a Van Dyke. He was dressed in a bright colored shirt, not exactly an African dashiki, but close enough to proclaim him to be of some artistic association with African culture. He wore sandals. And the little John Moore heard of his language was clothed in a pronounced English accent. The woman referred to him as Juliet . . . or did John Moore hear Julian? She wore too much of what people more than forty years old would call rouge. Her hair was processed, and it sat untidily on her head. Her jaws were fat. Her lips were fat, and held in a constant pout. There was grey hair on her chin, not enough to be called a beard. The silk in her dress, and the cut it was subjected to, made her look rounder than she was. She spoke with an American accent. All the accents he heard when he first arrived sounded native. But now that he had heard some conversation at shorter distance and with three badly sitting scotches, he was recognizing the foreigners at this cocktail party. There were lots of them.

They were walking along a path, cemented and bordered by vines of bougainvillea on green-painted wooden arches, and then they turned into an open patch of lawn where there were bird baths of white cement, empty, in one of which someone had rested an empty plastic glass.

Weekesie stopped immediately behind a man, and said softly, "Rev!" When the man turned around and faced them, he was pushing three dainty trimmed sandwiches into a large mouth. His lips were very thick, and they gave the impression that he was always pouting. How ironical those lips on a man of the cloth! He wore a wooden crucifix on his long flowing black cassock. He wore something around the neck which looked like a cape. This cape and portions of the black cassock were trimmed in red.

"Hi there!" the Reverend said. There was a gob of chewed-up sandwich sticking to the line of gold-filled upper teeth. He looked so relaxed in this company. He was so much a part of it that his clerical attire had obviously not been conspicuous. John Moore had seen the man, or rather the attire, when he had first arrived; but he had dismissed it as someone in costume. After all, the tropics was a place where carnival was part of the way of life. The man referred to as Juliet by the round-faced lady was himself dressed as if he were leaving the cocktail party to attend a masquerade party. There were so many strange things which he had seen and had been confronted with in his short stay that this man could have been masquerading as a man of the cloth.

"Meet the new Director of National Culture," Weekesie said. This was the first anyone had called him by his full official title. And it was said in its proper place, with its proper force; and it sounded very foreboding and important like the newspaper article had reported. It sounded like a job which he could not be happy with, because of its obvious power. Power was new to him.

"Welcome," the Reverend said.

"The Reverend Lionel Lipps. The Rector of Saint . . ."

Just then, before John Moore heard the name of the church, a loud laugh exploded all over the lawn. It had come from a corner of the lawn where the bougainvillea were thickest and reddest and most luxuriant. The man called Juliet was holding back his white bearded head, and was laughing. One hand he held on his flat belly. It seemed like a careless expression of emotion. The man was laughing too loudly for a cocktail party of this kind. For if what Weekesie had been saying could be taken seriously, then the country had become a place in which each action and word had to be thought out carefully before its expression; and the known and unknown repercussions understood clearly beforehand. This loud behavior could bring the man into lots of trouble, unless of course he was a man so rooted to the people with power that he didn't have to care. But he did not look like a man who was independent and powerful. His flamboyant quality of dress and the color of his clothing made him look effete. Imagine wearing sandals with his unclipped toenails exposed at a cocktail party like this!

The Reverend Lionel Lipps, Rector of Saint . . . peered over the rim of his two-tone tortoise-shell spectacles, and beneath his breath, uttered a curse. "Jesus Christ! Some civil servants don't have any blasted civili-

ty in them, at all!" The butler came by just then with a
tray of drinks, and close behind him was a beautiful
black woman carrying a plate of small golden fried balls
which looked like fish cakes, or potato balls. The
Reverend Lionel Lipps helped himself to a glass of
scotch and water, and remembered in time, before the
butler walked off, to drink some in the glass in his hand,
and pour another glass into that. He smiled at the
woman. The gold in his teeth showed. And between
them still was chewed-up paste of the previous sandwich. He said, "Sister, how are you?" And as if she had
been blessed by him, she smiled back and waited, knowing his eating habits, until he had stuffed his mouth with
four of the balls, and then taken six more in his hands.
"Certain persons in this country never will learn proper
deportment. Suppose the Prime Minister was here!" The
Reverend Lionel Lipps had put so much awe and fear
into his voice that the seriousness of the other man's
laugh, in the present circumstances, became obvious
even to John Moore. To him, the laugh and the possible
breach of manners had to be understood as only a laugh.
But to the Reverend Lionel Lipps it was something more
deplorable. "Something has to be done about that type
of behavior," he said. He had changed his facial expression from pleasant satiety, and had transformed it into
one of a fire-breathing evangelist. His thick lips
appeared miraculously thinner, his cheeks were now
drawn in, and he was shaking his head in disbelief at the
breach of protocol. "I shall certainly bring this to the
Prime Minister's attention," he said. It was as if the man
who had laughed had already been chastised, punished,
and prohibited from attending more of these cocktail
parties for life; as if no one present would stake his reputation to include this man's name on any other cocktail-
party list, so impressive and final was the threat. The
Reverend turned towards them, and added, "You know,

every Sunday morning at seven o'clock, me and the Prime Minister meet to discuss the political situation and certain things about security. I provide him with all the feedback he needs. Well, on Sunday coming, I shall have to tell the Prime Minister what happened here this evening."

It was unbelievable.

Weekesie had fallen significantly silent. The Reverend imposed his personality on all those around him. He was making it plain, through his associations, that he was not a man to be ignored. He was smoking his pipe now. He looked quite full and contented. Smudges of saliva, almost dried, were at the corners of his mouth, and it looked as if the intake on the pipe was leaking spittle. His jaws were clamped firmly over the small stem of the small pipe; and he was sending puffs of smoke like declarations of power and judgment over the man who had dared to laugh. But he was not really thinking about the man now. He had spoken, as he would have spoken in the pulpit on a packed Harvest morning, on Easter Sunday; and he knew that his words would be listened to, if not obeyed.

John Moore started to think of other reverends he had known. There was one, a white man, but native born, who liked to drink enormous quantities of the local drink, "mauby." But this man whose name was Pembritton was a more sophisticated version of the Reverend Lionel Lipps; less a figure of ridicule, less a character from a comedy play. When the Reverend Lipps was first introduced, he wanted to laugh because he was an unbelievable character. A joke. And he wondered what it was about him that made him so ridiculous. Now he knew. The Reverend Lionel Lipps was a spitting image of that other man of the cloth, Reverend Pembritton. Perhaps the Reverend Lionel Lipps realized this; had always revered the real man as his model; and in his student days at the college, where he studied Canticles and Epistles and other religious teachings, had subconsciously copied more than he had intended.

"Do you remember a man named Pembritton? ... "

Weekesie took him aside. The lady with the round red face with the single hair of beard had come up to speak with the Reverend. Weekesie said to him, "You realized that too?"

"But Pembritton is dead, isn't he?"

"He is living. Just look at Lipps."

The man with the white beard was laughing again; this time, less noisily.

"Lipps is a joke. He's what we call a *yardfowl.*"

"Yard fowl?"

The language was strange; but even in this strange usage, he was able to detect something detestable, something despicable in the meaning of the term. Perhaps it meant that Lipps was a man who picked up corn from the ground. And since the fowls walked on the ground, on the same ground where the corn was thrown, then his mouth would most likely be tainted by some of the fowls' droppings. But Lipps was obviously a man. He was not a fowl. And a fowl, certainly the complete term, *fowl-hen,* was a woman. The term might mean, he reasoned, that Lipps and others, perhaps thousands of others in the country, were like women, waiting for the crow of the cock. But who was the cock of the walk? The Prime Minister? If it meant that, if that was its inner meaning, then "yardfowl" was the most uncomplimentary term one man could use to describe another man.

"People don't talk anything political when Lipps is around," Weekesie said. "But what is more serious than that, is that it says something damn serious about the people who run this country, when they run it on feedback and gossip. Could you imagine a government making decisions on this kind o' information, and making policy decisions . . . "

"But does he really, can he really just call up and go and see the Prime Minister, and talk about that man who laughed, just like that?"

"Man, this whole fucking country is run off information from yardfowls. They call it "feedback.""

"And he would repeat what happened here?"

"The Prime Minister listens to smaller things than that. The Prime Minister hears *everything*."

"About all the parties in the country?"

"Political parties?"

"Cocktail parties."

"Are you worried? The way things are in this country, a party is a party. It doesn't make any difference."

John Moore had come home with the firm belief that his country was unlike all the other new independent countries. In some of them, there was a distinct voluble clash between the rich and the poor, the white and the black. In others, people were talking about black power, and other versions of black nationalism. In one other country, there was the question of the Rastafari cult. What did his country have? It was recently acclaimed "the freest country in the world." But the people who lived in it had to be careful how they talked, and how they laughed. And there was all this talk about the Other party. It was becoming clear to him that a man couldn't just open his mouth and laugh at a cocktail party. But there must be certain cocktail parties in the country where people did nothing but laugh.

"Look, man, you are home now. You've just come in. So, let's join the ladies over there by the oleanders, and fire some more liquor before you go to eat. The liquor is at least free."

There was a very beautiful woman standing close to him. Her hair was silk and shiny and was cut short. She was black and very beautiful. He had never seen a woman so beautiful in all his life. When he looked again, she was no longer there . . .

Weekesie was a permanent secretary in one of the government ministries. That meant he was a man of some substance. He lived in a house in one of the more exclusive developments. He had taken John Moore there, just after he had checked into his hotel. The "yard," as Weekesie called his house, was a three-bedroom bungalow-type structure made of concrete blocks. The high cost of labor in the country was so prohibitive, he said, that many people could no longer afford to build their dream houses out of the coral stone mined from the rock quarries, and used more generally in his younger days. "The banks own all these blasted new houses in this development, anyhow," he said. "No more coral stone, old man. Those old plantation houses and other houses of the local rich which were built like fortresses outta coral stone, all them days gone." The house was very impressive. "The banks would own me too, along with the blasted yard, if I didn't have a little thing on the side, a little touriss-business. Just a flat or two that I rent to the tourisses, you see what I mean?" The house had grounds that came from the front where a carport showed off an Austin Mini — for the wife, Weekesie said — and a Toyota Mark II, for himself; and it went in all directions from the bungalow, and ended at the precipice of a hill behind the house. The lawn was beautifully kept; and a wall of about four feet, painted white, protected the house from the others, which were built on the same pattern. There were flowers all round the property, all native flowers. They were planted inside the wall. There was not one garden bed planted in vegetables or fruits. In the back of the property was a swimming pool, the shape of a pear. Weekesie called this "my folly." After the quick tour of the property, Weekesie had taken a shower, changed his clothes, and after two quick drinks of scotch on the rocks, "for the road," they had left for the cocktail party. His wife was at work.

"And who is this charming young man you have been protecting all evening, Mr. Weekes?"

She was a tall woman. Her skin was smooth; and you could see about five inches of her light-brown skin around the middle of her body. And when your eyes left that part of her figure, and stretched down her thighs, you could see another three feet of one leg, exposed by the slit in the long skirt. Her hair was cut short, and was curly. It looked like a man's, and this effect somehow raised the feminine provocativeness in her. In Toronto he would have called her "mixed." But at home, here, she would be regarded as one of the sought-after light-skinned women. There was no emphasis here on blackness and beauty in women, so far as he could see. Another situation he must be careful to understand; and he must remember not to say stupid things like "blackness," and "black is beautiful." People didn't use these terms here. They might call him a radical for saying them. Weekesie had already warned him about his views on tourism. Most of his energy, he feared, would be taken up in remembering, for there was a razor-sharp protocol of behavior.

"Aren't you going to introduce us?" he heard the woman saying. The way she wore her dress and the sophistication in her manner were not native-conditioned. "Anyhow, darling, my name is Shirleigh, spelt S-h-i-r-l-e-i-g-h." She smiled. He saw the space between her two front teeth, on the top. His mind began to wander. There were certain local meanings associated with women who had such spaces between their teeth. "What is yours?"

"John Moore."

"Oh, Johnmoore!" Here again, his names were joined together. He was beginning to like the way it sounded. Perhaps he was a man with one name only: Johnmoore. "The new director of the *culture* of this great nation of ours! Shirleigh Harris's mine. Please to meet you, Johnmoore."

"That's the man!"

"We went to school together," she said. He suddenly recognized her face. The husky arrogant voice, so self-willed, was the same. Suddenly all those years were rolled back, and he remembered her voice as it had abused him once, in her refusal to meet his advances, with curt determination and not a little sauciness because of her higher social position at the time. Had she placed his face over all those years too? And was it his new position, which everyone so far seemed to be impressed by; was it his new social mobility which was singling him out, in his old society where place and privilege and a loan from Barclay's Bank — Dominion, Colonial and Overseas in those days — was almost impossible to get if you didn't already have place and privilege? The banks were filled with black people these days, Weekesie said. But she had belonged to the right family. She had always been somebody. He wondered whether she had married. Perhaps she had married some man, also from the right family, and had left him by the wayside when her enthusiasm for greater social standing conflicted with

his ability to procure it through increased salary or better connections. What had happened to him? She
looked like a woman who was looking for a man: a
solid man; not one of the available native men who
would know too much about her past. He became dis-
interested in her presence, and almost missed her invitation to join a group of her friends in the corner of the
lawn where the oleanders were beautiful.

"Do your thing, man," Weekesie said, as she
escorted John Moore away. "You are the star-boy now."
He said it like a black American, and then drifted away.
John Moore could not help marveling at the beautiful
flowers and the clean atmosphere and the clean air. He
could now understand why Canadian tourists usually
went wild with the beauty of the land, and called it paradise. He could feel himself as a tourist in this garden of
talk and oleanders and zinnias and beautiful women,
most of whom were over forty and grasping, but who
looked like twenty-year-old women.

"You saw how that man behaved?"

"Who is he?"

"That one there," she said, pointing out the white-
bearded man with the funny shirt. "He's always behav-
ing like a blasted homosexual. He doesn't have to tell
everybody that he's one. And he's not even a citizen!"

He wondered what she meant by that.

"Somebody will soon poison him."

"For laughing at a cocktail party?"

"Boy, there're more social murders committed in
this place than what John dreamed about." She had a
pleasant way of reverting to her native dialect, in the
midst of her formal speech, which was itself remarkable
because of the native color and intonation she put into it.
"I wanted to tell you something," she said, as if she had
immediately changed her mind about telling him.
"Everybody's watching you, so be careful. You have just

come back. The papers played it up. But it is so nice to see you after all these years!"

"Tell me something, Miss Harris . . ."

"Shir-leigh!" She smiled. "Or *Missis* Harris, if you have to."

"You're married?"

"Was."

"Were?"

"Ten years. To that loud-mouthed, homosexual man over there!"

"As I was saying . . . why do I have to be so careful, as you were saying?"

"Luckily, your mother's in New York, isn't she? Not even *her*, then." She smiled, and the space between her teeth glowed. "By ten o'clock this evening, this very evening, every word that you spoke here will be reported back to the Prime Minister. I understand that the government sent for you, right? Well, there're a lotta pimps right here, among us. You were just talking to one."

"*Weekesie?*"

Weekesie drove him back to the hotel, tired and hungry and confused. He did not want to enter any conversation with his friend. Too much had happened in such a short time. He could not accept the face value of what the woman had said, nor could he dismiss it as simple gossip. He was a stranger among his own people. He was becoming paranoid. And frightened. He had followed the violence and the play of power in other countries, and had put those things down to the egomania of the men who ruled in those countries. But he had not judged them, because he did not have to live in them. His country was, after all, "the freest in the whole world!" Any evidence he wanted to test the truth of this boast of freedom, he knew, would come into conflict with the power in the position of his new job. The power he felt he had was not a political power. If he were forced to think of himself as a powerful man, it would have to be through his poetry.

Weekesie started to say something, but realizing that his friend was tired, changed his mind.

John Moore started to think of his new appointment: he carried the minister's letter, written in green ink, in his wallet. That letter and that appointment were the final touches of recognition and acclamation of his success abroad.

"You know, old man," Weekesie was saying, "I envy you. I wish I had gone Away. Being a permanent secretary is really a dead end." He paused for a time, and they traveled some distance in silence. "I am at the top of my grade. There's nothing more to do, no way else to go. I'm fixed just there. So, what do people in my place do? What is there for a young man to do?"

John Moore wondered that perhaps somebody was using him to give the government some touch of class. And some intellectual glitter. Perhaps the minister who had written the letter wanted to be an internationally known poet himself. Perhaps the government, like a medieval oligarchic monarchy, was bringing together into its palaces, in time for the coming Independence celebrations, all the best artistic brains, to give sophistication and culture and style to the new country.

"That is why so many civil servants, like myself, are into the tourist thing," Weekesie was saying.

John Moore hadn't heard much of what he was saying, he was so tired and confused with his own ruminations. But he tried to sit up and be attentive. If the society was riddled by rumor and gossip, then a man like Weekesie would know what was being said about him, and by whom. So he did not want to give him the impression that he, too, had succumbed so early to this vicious tongue-wagging.

"Do you really like living here?" he asked Weekesie for no reason at all.

"*I love* living here, man." He seemed ready to talk. "As the ordinary people say, '*I just loves living here.*' Man, I love living in this country so much that I always have my Canadian passport in my jacket pocket."

"But why?"

He took it from his jacket, like a prized possession, like a passport to two worlds of behavior and possession. "I am not in a minority on this, yuh know. A lot of people here, including top civil servants, have multiple-purpose visas to America and Canada. Everybody in power, almost all the businessmen in this country, either have two passports, one o' them being a Canadian passport, or else an American visa. And if you could get a straight answer from *anybody*, anybody at all, and ask them what they would like most to do, the first thing they will tell you is *'Leave!'* He slowed down the car, leaned towards John Moore and said, "Between me and you . . . in strictest confidence . . . even the Prime Minister have one o' these, so they say." He was waving his Canadian passport in John Moore's face.

They fell silent again. They had been driving for some time, for some distance. It was like traveling somewhere and going nowhere. John Moore had remembered nothing of this section of the country. It had become quite dark now. In this part of the world, the sun says a sudden farewell, and the land is overtaken immediately by the darkness. He remembered this time of day as the time when he had to ramble over the hill to find the sheep which his mother kept to supplement her family's nutrition and income, and cut the grass burnt by the sun from the stubs along the sides of the hill for the sheep to eat during the night. Did sheep eat during the night? Or was that just another untutored belief among the poor farmers? And after that, he had to help with the evening meal. And then there was homework from school. He remembered the Latin exercises, which always bothered him: he would sit before the kerosene lamp and watch the lampshade get blacker and blacker, and notice in his fatigue from studying, and from the housework, that the piece of brown paper, used before by the shopkeeper to wrap bread and salt beef and flour and salt fish, which he attached to the shade to beat the poor light exactly down on to the intractable Latin prose of Tacitus, was smoking; and perhaps if he did not stop nodding, the smoke would find them in the snoring bedroom behind him, in that licked-out bedroom of father and mother, and the house would erupt on fire; and the darkness outside then, twenty years ago, would engulf him, like the darkness of strangeness and intrigue that was engulfing this Toyota Mark II, in which he was traveling with a friend from those same days whom the woman had called a pimp. They drove now down the oily hill wet from the sudden rain, past a red building which used to house soldiers and sailors, presumably from the Boer War. Not that there was ever a Boer War in his country, or in any other country for all his tender knowledge knew; it was just that the term "Boer War" was used then to connote antiquity. They passed this romantic building from their past, down through a half-finished road where the houses were unpainted and small and dilapidated.

"Elections in the air, old man!" Weekesie said. "The minister fixing this road, at last!"

"Your ministry?"

"No, not my ministry."

John Moore did not press the point. Instead he tried to reason: How does it feel every long day in the bright equalizing sun to have to pass through this area with its smell of the ghetto before you could reach a tourist hotel, or a three-bedroom ranch-type bungalow; or was the passage of big imported automobiles through this canal the same as ships passing in the night, not recognizing each other's presence?

He could barely see the figure of a woman through the divisions in the wooden paling of a backyard as she held an enamel basin in her hand and threw lumps of thick stuff on the ground. And immediately, the waddling noises of fat ducks jumping on the porridge of "mash," as the local people call it, and wallowing in it. A child was in the next house. He held almost half of his small black body through the open front door, almost blocking the glare of the kerosene light, and cried out something. He could not understand the child's language. The child could be calling mother or father, or even the chickens next door. There were chickens rushing, before all the light in the house was snuffed out by the index finger and the thumb, and the day was emptied. And just beneath the shirt of the child was the round fullness of belly, and a short, not quite straight penis, from which dripped in lazy drops, like physical morse code, some message to the lapping dog at the front step. The front step was a blackened coral stone. They used to build mansions, in days ago, with coral stone. Remember? The color of this stone now told you that perhaps generations have stepped on it, as the governments have stepped on these people in this area, to get in and out of this time, and in and out of this house. "Elections in the air, old man!" And the coral stone tells you, too, that this house has not progressed at the same rate as the rest of the country.

The magnificence of the hotel came up in front of them, and this brilliance of lights and the faint rhythms of music took his mind off the coral stone. "Well," Weekesie said, getting out and coming round to open his door. "Been a damn long day!"

"Thanks."

"One o' these days, no big thing, I have something to show you. You might find them interesting."

"What?"

"Pictures. Photos. I already got a laugh out o' them. They're no use to me anymore. But you are a newcomer . . ."

He tried to place the chair that stood so proudly in the most conspicuous position in the hotel lobby into context. He had seen a similar chair somewhere else, in a more significant time. Now he remembered. It was a chair similar to the one in which Bobby Seale, the Black Panther leader, had chosen to have his photograph taken, during the radical sixties. Who sits in this chair in this country? He wanted to sit in it, and have his photograph taken. But the gesture might be misunderstood. Who had placed such a powerfully symbolic chair in the lobby of such a respectable hotel? There might be no significance attached to its place here. The land was not famous for its quoting of history, even when that history touched its people. Things were done, were praised in the heat of the moment of their commission; and then were forgotten. This chair was therefore just a beautiful chair to them. Just as the land was beautiful.

He walked out and got into a taxi. The street was deserted. It was one of the busiest daytime centers of small business. In this street there were men pushing hand carts with lumber to be delivered four or five miles out of the city on the sweltering soft tar roads; and there were women sitting, fat and without shape, either naturally or through the way they had to sit on the makeshift benches. Most of them wore a kind of hawker's uniform: dressed with no regard to fashion or style in old shoes, and broad-brimmed hats to shield them from the broiling sun, they sat in front of their trays of fruits; the fruits rotting gently in the sun; vegetables wrinkled through the age of the day; or fish, if it was late in the afternoon. The best-dressed women would be selling confectionery: "sugar cakes," and roasted peanuts, and in these days of progress and tourism, Wrigley's chewing gum. All this was the daytime scene. And all the talk among these hawkers was about the coming elections. The poor people did not seem to care who heard their political views. They seemed to understand that the Prime Minister's wrath at their increasing disloyalty could not make them any poorer; and so they continued to say that the government was as bad as the Other party. He tried to remember this street, and other streets in the city, through which the taxi was taking him now to meet the woman. She had called and had asked him to meet her. There was a lot of noise from impatient motorists and cyclists and the hundreds of pedestrians who used this street in the daytime. The stores and shops along this street sold everything from used furniture to rum and fried fish, and lunches for the laboring men who worked in the warehouses with the foremen who were local white men. These white men went on dressing out of season and out of the present independent times, in white suits, and one or two of them wore the lingering cork hat to remind the progressing blacks of the city that they were still, in spite of independence, the avoirdupois and control of the country . . .

He tried to remember. And the taxi driver — he too seemed to be remembering something; the way he was talking made no sense of clarity and present reality, so he must be remembering: " . . . *So you see, Mr. Johnmoore, there was this man, you see, a real educated man, a man who was a scholar of the classical laguages, who used to write some real good things about democracy in this country in the local newspaper, and the things he used to write had the people thinking. His name was Brian Pond, but people called him just Pond, Pond, and I not going to mention his name again, 'cause telling you all this could get me in trouble, not only with the government but with a lot o' other people in this country; you know, Mr. Johnmoore, in this day and age, a man can't always talk what he know to be the truth, and this is a day and age where the truth does not always be able to set you free; for as a matter of fact, there was a man like the one I telling you about, and he talked the truth and nothing but the truth in court one day at ten o'clock and by four o'clock that very said evening he was locked up like a common criminal, which is a sheer case of the truth not setting a man free. But I am telling you, though, Mr. Johnmoore, about this man who knew classical languages, and you know, one day something happen; but I not going to tell you what that something is, or was, because that would be worse than telling the truth; but all I am going to tell you is that there is a saying going-round the country now to the effects that 'The Lord giveth and the Lord taketh away,' and no matter how often I repeat that rhyme to myself, it don't make complete sense, it don't make rhyme or reason to me. I is not of course a educated man, but I been driving tourisses in this place for donkey years, and in my simple way o' looking at things and tourisses I was forced to see that all the money they bring-in in here, don't ever reach-down to people like me; and if I was you, with that big job you have, the first thing I would do is stop the blasted tourisses from coming here in droves. The only thing that the tourisses bring here to this country is chewing gum and high-heel shoes that you see all the young men wearing nowadays, and a lotta other slackness, and if you call that democracy, then I prefers a republic of the few; 'cause I drives taxis as I told you, but what is in it for me? Not one blasted thing, save a few dollar-bills, and every year the dollars getting more smaller and going more shorter, and the big hotels eating-up every-damn-thing, and they even start running their own transportation service from the airport . . .*

"... and lemme tell you something else, Mr. Johnmoore, before I put you off at your stop ... Man, me and my buddy just missed throwing a six-love in some fella's arse, arguing over a domino-game, over you and in your behalfs, man! Yes! One side o' the fellas start talking a lotta shite that this country is too small to have its own independent culture, and they start calling you a radical for coming to build-up the culture, and I had was to start cussing bad bad bad in defense o' you, man."

"Seems as if everybody knows I'm here."

"Man, how you mean? You was in the papers for almost a week, front page, man! And too, yuh see, Mr. Johnmoore, me and your father was gamblers together in the young days . . . This is where I letting you off."

John Moore gave him the fare, and as he knew he had to, a large tip. The information given, although not asked for, still had to be paid for. He was learning fast. A bond had been created. Some day he might have to call on this taxi driver for help. The taxi driver understood all this.

"And Mr. Johnmoore, if you don't mind my saying so, you are meeting a damn fine lady. I recognize her from the car license, and I knew her father too!"

"You know Mrs. Harris?"

"Man, yuh can't hide nothing in this country. That is why I advise you, as a man in a big important position, to tell the truth, if you was listening to my argument. It can't always set yuh free, the truth, but be-Jesus Christ, as your father uses to say, nobody can't put a gun to your head, and make you leave the place you was born in, 'cause you borned right here, like that fella I started-out telling you about, Pond. Have a nice night, son . . . and remember Pond . . . "

What a place he had come back to! You never know how free you are, he was thinking on his way to work for the first day, you never know how free you are, how much freedom you have living in an alien society, until you come back to your own free and independent country. The woman had offered to take him to work this morning. He felt that she would want to take him every morning after this. He must be careful with this woman.

"What a nice place have I left to come back here!"

"What a place you come to now, boy, if you don't mind me call you a boy. I know you Northamericans don't like that term. What a place you picked!"

"Tell me, who is this Pond that everybody is talking about?"

"What do you want to know?"

"I've heard about him more than once already. A taxi driver was telling me about him, the first night I met you."

He glanced at her, to see what her reaction would be; and he was in time to see that she had become tense: perhaps with the weight of the information she had. He was beginning already to regard her as a dangerous woman: a woman who knew her way too well. He had never before become willingly involved with an intelligent, worldly and sophisticated woman, as this one seemed to be. She made him feel uncomfortable.

"You didn't discuss it with him, did you?"

"Of course not!"

"Good." She was handling the car like a man, as they say. "Pond. Byron Pond. He was a lawyer." He waited to see if she was going to say more about Mr.

Byron Pond. "Can you remember those days when we were going to school, and the whole place used to be cheering for you, and urging you on? And you made all of us feel as if we had come first, like you always used to do?"

"That was thirty years ago."

"Thirty years! In that time I got married, had three children, got divorced, and built a new living for myself."

"I couldn't bear to come second. Do you realize that I've never come second in my whole life?"

"You can't be that ambitious here, though. While you're home now, try not to come first. They won't like you for that. Down here, you see, a strange thing has been happening. Down here, Johnmoore, people kill one another to come second. Second-place is admirable here. The people in this country, the people who run it too, don't want nothing more than second. The government wants second place. And the ministers all want to be known as the *second most powerful man* in the country. You will never hear a minister in this government say he wants to be prime minister, that he wants all the power. You know, Johnmoore, I think that they are all satisfied to have people call-out at them as they drive around in their Mercedes-cars, 'Look, man, look at the minister! The second most powerful man in the country, man!' I really think so."

"You must be kidding!"

"No, man. Listen. We came second in Miss World Beauty Contest last year. And the celebrations for that second-place, man, Johnmoore, you would've think that we had won the *duckey!*" She laughed, an almost vulgar laugh; and the space between her teeth was exposed; and he thought he saw all the heart of her sensuality exposed with it. "I won't mind being the second most powerful woman living here!"

"Who is the most powerful?"

They were entering the driveway of the building where his office was.

"When you go back up North, you will see her there . . . if the bitch ain't dead yet!"

"A white woman?"

She stopped the car right in front of the main entrance of the building. Some of the officers were arriving; and some who had recognized him lingered at the door, to see if they recognized the woman he was with, on his first morning, and perhaps put two and two together, and spread a new rumor. She noticed them staring, and touched him on his leg.

"You know something? I think you need me to take care of you," she said without a smile on her freshly made-up face. He could not see the space between her teeth.

That same beautiful black woman he had seen first at the cock-tail party appeared close to him now. Her eyes were like devils, large and naughty. Her face was angelic and small for the size of her body. He had not seen such enticing lips before . . .

He looked through the window of his office, forcing his eyes to see beyond the luscious bush of the trees planted outside the window, into the space between two cars, where a man was standing talking to another. He thought he recognized the man; had seen him some-where before. He shuddered slightly from the air condi-tioning. It was the first time he had ever had an office and a private secretary, and this unaccustomed power was making him uncomfortable. It was the first time he had ever been in charge of anybody. His staff numbered two hundred. The minister who had written him the let-ter inviting him to take the post had called earlier that morning to welcome him.

"I don't know how you're going to do it, but that place up there needs cleaning out. There is great ineffi-ciency, and after two acting directors, we can't seem to get the damn place straightened-up. Well, welcome, and good luck. But as I say, I don't envy you. Let's meet soon for lunch." And when he hung up John Moore was even more uneasy.

He had been told by friends who had never left the country, and who had somehow climbed into the ranks of the new native management elite class, that his staff, even the senior staff, was the "worst bunch o' bastards" ever collected in one place. They warned him that they would be coming to him with all kinds of problems which had nothing to do with their jobs, and that the place was a bed of rumor and corruption. He just nodded and thanked them for their advice, and concluded that they were overstating the problem.

Oliver Golding was one of this new black management elite. He had spent seven years in Toronto studying business administration at Ryerson Polytechnical Institute; and, before he had left to return home, had worked in a large firm as a senior executive. He had liked it in Toronto, as had his wife, now home again with him, in a large cement-block bungalow, in social and economic circumstances far beyond her wildest expectations had they remained at home. She had been sitting comfortably on the couch which they had imported from Canada; and had been saying what she would do, and would not do, to get back to Toronto.

"Those lovely winter nights — I just love them." She was drinking brandy. That too had been imported. She said she had developed a taste for brandy during the long winter nights when Oliver was studying for his degree in business administration. "I just love the way you have to dress in Canada, you know? Like in the summer, you wear different clothes, and I just love the winter wear. Those lovely winter leather boots and the furs. And down here, what do we have? The same damn thing twelve months a year. No variation at all in life." She looked at her husband, fat and shining from his new prosperity and position in the community, and she smiled. Her smile said she was nevertheless thankful for her present position; and for his. He understood, he said, her yearning to get back to the big city. But he had a contribution to make to his country. "No damn variation at all," she said, with the proper sophistication wrapped around the emotive word. "In this place, you get up, you eat, you rest in the afternoon, and you go to parties every night, all night, and you meet the same people. And the men all want to take you to bed, and would say so, even in front of your husband; and the women, the wives, are all bastards and bloody dull." She sipped her drink. She could have been in Toronto right for that moment. "It's nice, though, to live among your own people, after seven years in Canada. But it gets me depressed, sometimes. If I could only make Oliver make up his mind . . . "

"Man, listen to her!" Oliver said. He had just returned from looking after their young son who had the television playing too loudly. The son could not be dragged from the television set. It was his first real gift, for his ninth birthday; and it was a color set, "a colored set" the wife had said, smiling; and the majesty of the color had entranced him. "Man, I telling you, see. Being home is a funny thing. Particularly after you spend time in Canada being trained, and then come back. Nobody want to regard you as a man. Because they know where you come from, they remember you when you were growing up in this place. And they don't like that kind o' change and progress in a poor person. And they will always remind you of what you were when you were going to school, and who your father is. And if you didn't attend the college, there's a whole life not exposed to you. They won't let you in to that club, not for shite! This country hasn't changed, man. That really gets me. I've been back now for four years. It took me the first three years to get to know these people all over again. From scratch. It's tough, man."

John Moore could not, at that time, see the problems he was alluding to; in fact, he did not see the problem of adjusting. The problem he had was in making his staff work.

He had found out that in the past his staff used to take three hours or so away from their desks, away from the office building, for lunch. Assignments were never handed in on time; and there were always flimsy excuses made. And no reprimands. He and Oliver knew that in Toronto, a man was not given too many chances to prove that he deserved the job he was hired to do. But it was different here. Their experience abroad implanted in them the idea that a new, young, small developing country could be a good challenge. One could do so many things here. All the new techniques, both of living and of working, could be applied here. And the country, poor as it was, with its monumental unemployment and scarcity of skilled and professional people; the country, like its people, would be glad, should be glad for these time-saving, money-saving techniques.

"Lemme tell you something, see. It don't work so, here!"

And Oliver related what he considered to be the most remarkable incident in the early days of his management. It was a story of ignorance. *"Now, listen. One day I walk into the plant, where my people are wrapping bread. And I walked and stopped beside this woman. And there she was, eating Kentucky Fried Chicken and wrapping bread at the same time!"* He liked telling this story. He said that no way could that have happened in Canada. No way could she have got her paycheck after that. "But here? Man, I fired her, and the whole Workers' Union came down on my arse because I said it was unsanitary. And only after they nearly closed-down the blasted place, did I really think that that woman could *in no way* understand what she was doing." He took a long sip of his scotch on the rocks. "And that is what I mean, when I tell you about these people and change. Change? Jesus Christ, this place likes change like the Mafia loves the Royal Canadian Mounted Police!"

His private secretary was standing before him now; and must have been there for some time, for he had been taken back to that night when he and Oliver tried to change, in one night, all the attitudes of the country. His secretary remained standing as he looked at her. He did not like this woman at all: there was something about her that made him uneasy; she looked like a mouse in mouse's clothing, a kind of old-fashioned prudishness covered her face, and she too wore rouge on her cheeks, which had many small black moles; too many to be mistaken for beauty marks.

"There's a gentleman to see you, sir."

"Who is he?"

She fumbled a little as she stood, and realizing that she would have to know the man's name before he would be admitted, she turned and went back into the outer office, where he could hear her saying to the man, "He want to know who you are. Who should I tell him you are?"

When the man came in, John Moore recognized him as the same man who had laughed at the cocktail party. He was wearing a bright-colored shirt, outside the trousers, similar in design and style to the one he had worn then; white trousers, sandals.

"I'm not taking up your time, am I?" He waited to be invited to a chair, and as he sat, John Moore saw that he was a man of about forty-nine or fifty-five years; he was much older than he looked, and the clothes he wore, apparently chosen to cover his approaching retirement age, could do nothing for him when it came to sitting down. "I'm not intruding, am I? I know how it is when you begin a new job." His white beard was immaculately clipped and shaped, and he sat in the chair in such a way that he looked like a man who had some army experience behind him. "You know, I saw you at that diplomatic party that afternoon, Sah; but I just couldn't get over to greet you and welcome you back home. Jolly-good-to-have-you-back-among-us-Sah! I've followed your career. Yale, wasn't it? And Harvard, Brandeis, Smith College, Princeton and bless-my-soul-Sah, you didn't despise the Deep South . . . Duke University, damn good institution, famous for ESP, and then Texas, among the Longhorns!"

John Moore was smiling now. Somebody in this country knew about him.

"I'll come to the point, Sah. Do you have a place in your organization for a man like me? I know you've just started, and there are things you'll want to look at first. But I am desperate." This man was at least fifteen years older than John Moore, and that difference in age, added to the request, was a bit unbalancing. The man saw this, and could do nothing about it. "Oh, I didn't tell you who I am. I'm Harris, Juliet Harris. They call me Julie. I think you went to school with my wife. My ex-wife, that is . . . "

"But I thought you were . . . "

"That's just it. If I may tell you the circumstances of my disposition, my present disposition, that is, Sah . . . you see, I am a man who lost his job because of . . . what should I say, an indiscretion."

No one should call a man so proud-looking and so dignified by a name such as Julie, John Moore was thinking, as the man talked. "I-have-to-be-honest-with-you-Sah, that's-my-policy. Honesty. Learned it in the army, I did."

This was the very first person he was interviewing for a job, and he didn't know what questions to ask; he didn't know what to do. This man, obviously more intelligent than he, brought to this state because of "an indiscretion." He wanted to ask him what indiscretion; but he was too embarrassed to do that. And he didn't even want the man to continue. It was very painful to look at him . . . this man could have been his father, except for the flamboyant shirt and the trimmed Van Dyke beard. He looked through the window, trying to find the same space between the thick bushes and the two cars parked outside. The woman with the space between her teeth was meeting him for lunch . . . it would be good to be with her, at a quiet table, having a few drinks, near the sea . . .

"I'm asking you to see if you could do anything for me, man, I am begging you! I am begging you. They fired me this morning. Fired me. And for what? For laughing-out at a cocktail party! Man, that's a big joke, in a democratic country! 'You did not have the proper deportment and respect of protocol,' they say. Man, tell me if this is the twentieth century . . . " Tears were in his eyes now. And his body looked even older, and tired. The flamboyant shirt was now a drooping flag covering his shaken body. His voice became high-pitched, almost hysterical, laughing and crying out at the same time, "They fired me after twenty-five years' service, because I laughed-out at a cocktail party! Man, you don't think that is a lotta shite!" He had expressed and exposed all his emotion; and now there was no more need for this debasement of himself; and he realized this, and pulled himself together, and was almost his former self. "Forgive the emotional display, Sah . . . one-of-those-things. I thought you could be of some assistance . . . " What was the woman going to wear for her lunch date with him? "Well, I-shall-be-getting-out-of-your-way, you're a busy man, Sah. I thought you could help, I thought you could help . . . "

John Moore got up with him, and walked to the door, as the man stood at attention, militarily and with respect in his posture. John Moore promised to help him, and he told him to leave his telephone number with the secretary. The man thanked him; and just as he went out, he paused and turned, still as if he was on a parade square, and said quite neutrally, "The Lord giveth and the Lord taketh away . . . "

The secretary came back in, and stood before him. She irritated him when she stood like that. He quickly, there and then, devised a plan for dealing with her: he would pretend that she was the woman who ate Kentucky Fried Chicken and wrapped fresh bread with the same hands: ignorant.

"Mrs. John, what can I do for you?"

"I have typed the letters."

"What letters, Mrs. John?"

She moved slightly, uncomfortably, from one leg to the other. She put a very submissive, scolded expression on her face.

"But I didn't give you any dictation this morning ... "

"Well, you see sir, these are the three letters you dictated to me four days ago. I was very busy and I couldn't always follow my notes, and I only had a chance to do them today."

"Thank you very much, Mrs. John."

She placed the letters, contained in a red leather folder marked "For Signature," before him, and moved sedately out of the office, closing the door quietly behind her. She moved as if she was leaving the room of a sick person. They said that her husband used to be a minister in the Church, but he had died recently, leaving her a very young child with whom to mourn her former protected life.

He looked at the folder, put it directly in the middle of the green blotting paper pad, and went back to thinking of the previous evening's conversation and drinks at the Oliver Goldings'. "This is the way things are in this place, see," Oliver had said. It was as if Oliver was warning him not to be too ambitious in his job. But he couldn't understand why it had to be this way. Didn't the country, and the government and the people themselves, realize that this national inefficiency was not a virtue? *This is the way things are in this place, see.*

He took the For Signature folder from the blotting paper, and held it in his hand. He couldn't remember to whom he had written; he didn't remember the letters. There had been so many letters he had dictated during the short time he had been director of culture. Now that it was on his mind, he could remember signing only five of them. But he must have given her more than five dictations in three weeks. He wrote more than ten letters a night to friends in Toronto and in Washington, D.C., and elsewhere; about half in his own hand, the rest typewritten. Everything here was done in such slow time. Now, what were these letters he had to sign?

One was to the National Funeral Directors' Association. Why would he be writing to funeral directors, anyway? A morbid thought came to his mind, and it involved his secretary. He glanced through the middle of the letter to see the reason he had to write them. He had made a speech in which he wondered aloud to his cigar-smoking businessmen's luncheon audience why it was still necessary for obituary notices to be read four times a day over the Government Broadcasting Service, GBS, in the time which should have been used for national culture. The funeral directors immediately regarded this statement as revolutionary, and he became their enemy; they wondered whether he "was not out of the country too long to know anything about the culture of funeral directing." He had then heard, through the normal gossip, that one of the country's leading directors wished him dead, and hoped that he would have the privilege of being responsible for his burial. "I would embalm that bitch in hot-oil and then throw him in the sea!" But he did not think that all of them had that sense of humor. The National Funeral Directors' Association was a group of very conservative, straight-laced and somber businessmen. In their official letter of protest to him, a copy of which they made sure to have published

in the daily newspaper, they had said, through their secretary, also an undertaker, that *"for someone who has lived
abroad for so long, as you have, sir, it is misleading to the people of this country for you now to come, as if from the grave,
and make these radical statements."* He had written to
invite them to a meeting in his office, at which the matter
would be cleared up; and this was one of the letters that
the secretary had just got around to typing. But it was
still only in draft form. He looked at the date he had dictated the letter, and saw that it had been given seven
days ago, not counting the weekend. He felt that his secretary was on the funeral directors' side: she might even
be related to one of them. The country was so incestuously bound by blood ties.

Her draft read: *"National Funerral Directors
Association, Dear Sirs, The Directer of National Cullture,
wishes to invite you to a meating with him, in his offices, on
the 7th instance. The Director is awaiting your replies on this
matter. Would you pleace inform him through his secretary, at
your earliest conveneince . . . "* Either she couldn't type, or
she couldn't spell; and he meant to find out before he
spoke to her about it. So he pulled out the bottom drawer of his desk. It was still cluttered. The previous director, an "acting director" as the minister in charge of this
department had called him, had left apparently in a
hurry; and he had left some of his papers in brown folders, with scratchy and illegible writing on them signifying their contents and their non-use. He could find no
order in that drawer so he tried the center drawer. In
this one were two bent, old, well-smoked and chewed
pipes; a few slides which had gathered dust (he looked
at a few of them and they showed naked women and
men at some party); and a magazine, *Yachting.* He was
searching to find the secretary's personal file. He wanted to see whether it was his personality which was causing the problem with her inefficiency, or whether she

was simply underqualified. He had been in the country long enough to know that "private secretary" had more to do with what the boss did with the secretary in private than with the secretary's efficiency. Mrs. John had been the previous acting director's secretary for five years. He found her personal file in the filing cabinet beside the side table. On the relevant page he read: "*Mrs. Monica M. John: Typewriting speed 30 words per minute; Shorthand 40 words a minute; Deportment very good indeed . . . Mrs. John came first in her graduating class. She previously worked as a secretary in the Prime Minister's office for two years and her work was excellent . . .* " He noted the name of the "academy" she had attended; and since the name made no sense to him, he closed the file and the cabinet, and put the For Signature folder into the wastepaper basket. The secretary might see it there, and remove it.

The telephone rang. It would be the woman, Shirleigh, calling about lunch.

"Well, how is it going so far?" It was the minister in charge. "Word has just come to me from the top, from the top. So I'm calling you to put you on your guard, just in case he comes looking for a position with you. Under no circumstances are you to take him on. That is the decision from the top. Of course, you realize this is quite confidential . . . in strictest confidence, you understand."

"I understand, Mr. Minister."

"Well, old man, having settled that little matter . . . Oh by the way! His name is Juliet, Juliet Harris. Not a bad fellow, but much too conspicuous, in a way. I assumed you knew who I meant. Forgot you're only back a short time. Now, the other matter. I want you to prepare a confidential report on indigenous culture. I can use this sometime . . . it will come in useful, sometime. Well, that's all for now. And remember that fellow, Juliet, would you?"

"Yes, Mr. Minister."

"I'll call you back shortly."

John Moore sat stunned to think that the wheels of power could act so swiftly and so harshly.

The telephone rang again. This time it was Shirleigh.

This is the way things are in this place, see.

He got up and left for lunch. It was only twelve o'clock.

On the way to a party some time after, in the early evening, he sat beside the woman, and tried to stay awake. He was having problems staying awake beyond seven o'clock. He had to attend so many lunches which lasted for two hours or more, and at which great quantities of liquor were drunk, including bottles of wine and liqueurs afterwards. His job did not call for physical exertion beyond that. "It could be the change in temperature and metabolism," the woman said. They were going to a party held by one of the "lady-expatriates," she said, "somewhere in the country district."

The road they took out of the city was a curving, winding one. He remembered how the tourist brochures advertised the country as having "the best communications system of well-paved roads in the world." His country was a country of superlatives. What a boast, he mused, fighting off the sleep. Sometime he would have to learn his way about; the time would come when he would disagree with this woman, and he would need to be able to drive himself. It was also good manners; each time they were together, it seemed he was dozing. But the car was moving easily along the road now, and he was glad to be in a relaxed, if slightly inebriated, state. He put his hand through the window, and the wind almost tore it off. He had no idea they were traveling so fast.

"Have you heard that the Other party is planning violence in the country?"

"Where do you hear all these things?"

He wanted to tell her about her ex-husband: that he had been fired from his job; but he would choose a more discreet time in which to tell her. It would be better, however, if it came from her first; in that way, he would know if she was really privy to everything that went on in the country, as was her boast. "The *Weekly* and the Other party are accusing the government about one-party states again," she said, and then, "How is your job?"

He told her about the secretary.

"You ain't seen nothing yet," was all she said. "They should try that foolishness up North. I worked as a secretary in New York when I was studying. Talk about *hard* labor?"

There was that beautiful smell again, of Lady-of-the-Night, and the heartening sight of people walking along the side of the road, which had no sidewalks, and no provision for them, as if they owned both the road and the country. They looked healthy, in spite of the high inflationary prices of food; and the women, most of them, were dressed well. The *Weekly* had said in a front-page article, last weekend, that malnutrition among the youths was at an all-time high. He did not even know that people had begun to measure such things. There was another article about the "high cost of things these days," and one in which the writer suggested that the government should hand over the "governaunce of this noble country" to the Other party. He satisfied himself that this nineteenth-century way of putting things was basic to the national humor.

The car pulled around a bend, and there before them, out of nowhere it seemed, was a large gathering. An exposed naked light blub glared stubbornly; and the people crowded around the light. Before he could ask her what kind of meeting this was, she offered to stop for a while; and she said, "If I had my way, I would lock-up all these blasted crooks. Calling themselves grass-roots! What this country needs is *money*, not more politicians."

So it was a political meeting. His excitement was aroused. She said the speaker was an ex-policeman; but that did not appear significant to him.

The speaker was a shortish man, well built, something like a boxer. He had shaven almost all the hair off his head. His face was round, but not childlike. It had rather a ferocious and pugnacious determination about it; and the way he was using his words, in the vernacular, was the way a Southern Baptist preacher would employ the jabs and uppercuts of revivalism and of brimstone warnings.

"I didn't come before you tonight to accuse this government o' corruption. And I ain't saying that this present government that we got, is the most corrupt in the history of this country. I am not saying that. But I saying tonight, ladies and gentlemen, that as a fellow I know, a friend o' mine who lives up in Brooklyn put it, 'Watergate don't have one damn thing on this place!' So, yuh can't accuse me, none o' you yardfowls and pimps in this audience, of brekking-up the Black Power Law, or the Security Law, or whatever the hell they calls it. And yuh know something? I don't even know the right name o' this law that they might use against me for talking to you tonight, simply because this government don't tell the people o' this country nothing. The people of this country don't know what goes on in the government. It is a secret government, brothers and sisters. A dictatorship government. A dictatorship of one man. And all you know who that man is! He isn' nothing at all. But lemme tell you something. A minister get up on a flatform two Friday nights ago, and say that he doesn't know anything about Pond. Yessss! A minister. He could get-up 'pon a flatform and make a statement like that. And when a taxpayer had the courage to ask why? . . . all he could say was that Pond did not discuss his business with him! He doesn't walk-'bout asking people their private business, he say. But I tell you something tonight, brothers and sisters, tonight I intend to blow the whole blasted lid offa all this government secrecy and one-party dictatorship. If a cabinet minister don't know what happened to Byron Pond, and Pond was a member o' the same cabinet . . . unless they got *they got two cabinets running this country! . . . tell me, how the hell would a common taxpayer like me or you know then? But as the whole country know, Pond was sent through the eddoes by the powers-that-be. They put a gun to Pond head, and drive him forth from the gates of the country in which he was born like you and me . . . drove him out of the gates of his country, and put him 'pon a airplane with a gun to his head, bound for Toronto. Well, I even seen him last month up in Toronto, then. And you know what I see Pond, a great out-standing son of the soil o' this country, you know what I see Pond doing? . . . Selling lead pencils on the corner o' Bathurst and Bloor Street . . . "*

A white man on the dark edge of the crowd asked the man standing beside him, "Tell me, what does 'gone through the eddoes' mean?"

"Shhhh! You can't hear the man talking politics?"

A woman standing beside the man, with her hand on the man's shoulder, said, "It mean 'fired.' Fired with disgrace."

"Thanks, madam."

" . . . and in case you-all don't know where Bathurst and Bloor is, in relation to the culture o' this country, well, anybody who ever went up on the fruit-picking cotton-picking labor scheme, could tell you that that is where the blacks does live, and lime and hang-out. This proud son of the soil. This brilliant scholar. A man able to read all kinds of world philoso-phies. And brothers and sisters, not only read philosophy in English, but read it also in Latin and Greek . . . and Hebrew! This man who came from the grass-roots like you. And me. This honorable gentleman, formerly an honorable member of the honorable House, this man was thrown to the goddamn dogs by the powers-that-be. They say that the Lord giveth and the Lord taketh away. So be it! So be it. A time going come when that Lord, whoever the hell he is, won't be Lord-and-master no more. So be it! But don't laugh, don't laugh, broth-ers and sisters . . . "

The crowd, apparently accustomed to this man's delivery, was breaking itself up in deep, belly-relieving laughter.

" . . . *because I am not a comedian. I am not like the ministers in this government . . . I come before you tonight as a serious politician. The comedians are in the government. A man from England even write a novel about the comedians who run this country. And I only mentioned that to say this. If a cabinet minister could stand-up 'pon a flatform and make misleading statements like that, then all o' wunnuh know where this country is heading. The political philosophy of this country, brothers and sisters, is 'Brek for yourself!' or in plain simple grass-roots language, 'Cover your own backside, because I ain' going cover it for you!' The Lord give wunnuh and the Lord could take it away. Big important civil servants lossing their jobs for nothing. One man I heard about just last night, loss his job because he laugh-out at a joke at a diplomatic party; and he didn't even give the joke himself. People getting lay-off, left and right. But I tell you something tonight, brothers and sisters, I telling you something tonight . . . I think I can hear poor Pond right now, wherever he is. Perhaps in some cold basement room up in Canada, where the temperature in the hottest part o' the winter does get as low as one hundred degrees below zero . . . but don't laugh, 'cause I am not a comedian. I am not one o' your cabinet ministers, so don't laugh at the politics I talking tonight. I talking grassroots politics . . . So that cabinet minister say that he doesn't comprehend what transpired in regards o' Pond? And he don't know what take place? Well, I can hear Pond, poor Pond sayin all this very-now, 'ELI, ELI, LAMA SABATHANI! . . . my God, my God, why hast thou sent me through the eddoes?' . . . Brek for yourself! . . . "*

"Who is that man?" he asked the woman, as they moved back to the car. He had never witnessed a man with such powerful control over a crowd. "That man is dangerous."

"The Lord giveth and the Lord taketh away, boy! You didn't hear him say so?" They had little difficulty moving through the crowd of several hundred people. "They call him Kwame. I can't remember his right name. Everybody knows him as Kwame."

He could hear the people breathing, as they listened to him; and he could hear, at least he told himself that he could hear, their breathing when the speaker ran with them along the rushing of the words that were like boulders coming down a hill. And now this explosion of breath came out as he reached the end of his poem. For it was a poem in the hands of his religious diction and skill. The speech had ceased to be a mere political harangue and had become a work of art . . .

That black woman with the blessed beauty was in the crowd
She was wearing an African necklace of either wood or bones,
brown and red and with some silver wire in it; and her neck
was long and soft. She watched the man with a raised head, as
if she knew that his words were meant particularly for her; and
for her alone. She was hidden in the laughing crowd . . .

The car was climbing a slight hill between two tall fields
of sugarcane, while he thought of what a dangerous man
he had just heard. They turned into a narrow unpaved
lane beside a small one-room school, and down the
steepness modified by large spreading breadfruit trees
and tall stringy green-pea trees; and then the car slowed
down to take a breath to climb the steepness beyond.
They came dangerously close to a public standpipe. A
man, bare down to his mildewed white drawers, taking
his evening bath under the pipe, straightened up; not so
much as if he was caught unawares in his lavatory, for he
made it clear through his casualness that he was on his
own territory, but rather as if he wanted to greet them,
and show them how happy he was bathing. And he
waved and said, "Good night, Mistress!" and went back
to washing his armpits, as if only a night bat had interrupted his bath. John Moore wondered why men in the
country districts greeted only the women, although they
were accompanied usually by men.

The car climbed the hill, and for a moment it was
like being in a plane, flying low, and at some incalculable
angle; and when he looked in the opposite direction,

through the egg of glass, he saw the skies disappearing. And then the car moved securely over gravel, through the stone pillars of a gateway that had no gate. And then there was the barking of dogs. And then a woman came out with her arms stretched to make the horizontal bars of a cross against the thickness of legs and African-print cocktail dress, and said, "About time!"

There was that tantalizing smell of Lady-of-the-Night, and the smell of other flowers whose names he must remember to find out from the woman, walking in her own fragrance of perfume. She gave him a pinch on his thigh, the only place her hand could touch in the darkness in the yard, and whispered, "Watch this old bitch!" and then smiled sweetly with their hostess. "I am so sorry, my dear, that we held you up. Gas, you know, petrol. And the damn thing is so dear these days! And to find a gas station open this time o' night . . . "

The hostess ushered them through a short passageway. They were walking on cool marble. On one side of this passageway, the wall was made of concrete blocks, decorated; and on the other, it was flat and rough. Then they entered perhaps the most artistically furnished and appointed house he had seen so far. Every last space of wall was covered with paintings. The floor was as slippery as it was clean. The hostess said it had been done that very afternoon by the maid, who came in "only to wash-up the dirty dishes and clean, which I have to do-over after her, anyhow;" and it shone and looked like dark rich mahogany. Standing there, he remembered his mother: she had worked for years scrubbing floors in a hotel.

"The roast cold. The rice cold. The salad wilting, but there's lots left back, though," she said, in her assumed vernacular. "What you drinking tonight? Come and fire one. Afterwards, I will introduce you to the gang."

Just then, a short, thick-in-the-waist, cocky-looking man with spectacles came out from the porch where the others were, and said, "Wait, wait, good-Jesus-Christ, I seeing right? I only just hear you in the land! When you get in? Come and fire one, man. Rum flowing like water, at this dinner party. Wait . . . " He had come from the other guests, who were looking up at the stars and down at the lights in the chattel-houses below, digesting their dinner of roast pork, doved peas, peas-and-rice, and salad made of avocado and cucumber. John Moore could see all this on the table beside which he was standing.

Without shaking hands, or introducing himself, the short man went up to Shirleigh and kissed her gently on her cheek, wrapped an arm around her waist tightly, and said, "Tek care o' that *hombre*, yuh! 'Cause your Ex gone through the eddoes. You hear?" John Moore was aghast at the man's casual cruelty. He could see Juliet sitting in his office with tears in his eyes. The woman simply smiled. He must find the right time to ask her.

They stood for a while examining the house: paintings and pictures on the walls, books in the tall bookcases, vast amounts of pottery on shelves; some pottery had been used for serving the meal which was still giving off a mouthwatering smell. Everything in this house had been carefully chosen, and carefully put into place, so that one got the feeling that here was perhaps the perfect arrangement of furniture and knickknacks. Even the *Weekly*, which was stretched half-open, had been carefully studied and placed to give the impression of casual intellectualism.

"I firing another one," the short man said, in a slow lazy way of speaking. He kissed Shirleigh again. "Shirl, you looking sexy as shite, yuh! This star-boy like he more better than Juliet, yuh!"

"You would know," she said. But it was obvious that the blush on her cheeks came there because of the embarrassment. John Moore again reminded himself to ask her about her ex-husband. "You ought to know, 'cause you're a minister. I wish you would learn to speak proper English, though." And she smiled.

"Girl, when yuh know it backwards, and yuh-can talk it in Latin on top o' that, yuh-can afford to handle it the way I handle it, which is the way the common-man does use it. I is a man from the people."

They followed the hostess out into the cigarette smoke climbing on the sheet of glass which protected them from falling into the valley, and from seeing what the people below had for dinner that night. The valley was beautiful. There were stars on one ridge, it seemed; and the lights in the small houses, which one could barely see in the valley cluttered with sugar canes and short trees; and the sea in the background.

A plane was coming in.

"Beewee!" somebody surmised.

"No, man. BWIA in already. Looks more like Pan-Am to me."

There were eight guests in addition to John Moore and Shirleigh. Two couples were introduced as Canadians. One man was referred to as a foreign representative. John Moore did not know if he worked for a Canadian multinational corporation, or whether he was with the Canadian High Commission. And then there was a mixed couple. Husband, white American; wife, black American. They told him the wife did things with local seashells and lacquer. The husband of this woman sat on the floor, between his wife's legs. The man referred to as "the Minister," and the lady on whose chair-arm he sat, were the only local people.

The conversation had been on the political situation before John Moore and the woman arrived. They returned to it now. "Boy, I give them hell, two-three nights ago 'pon a flatform up in the country," the

Minister said. He used the term "flatform," instead of "platform," just like the grassroots politician, Kwame. His slumbering pace of speaking changed imperceptibly into bravado. It seemed as if this Minister, after years of practice and politics, had deliberately decided to use the vernacular when dealing with the common people; and the condition had now become a characteristic. John Moore tried to make up his mind whether the man was speaking more like a minister in the Church, or a minister in the government.

"I went up there 'cause the party like it was in some kind o' trouble over Pond." Everybody in the room seemed to know who Pond was. "Nobody ain' listening even to the Prime Minister these days. And when he get up to talk, even in the House, people booing like hell. And Your-humble-servant was to go up there, in the lion's den, and throw some lashes in them. You shouldda hear the applause when I got through with them!" He was looking directly at the Canadian representative, whose attentiveness urged him on. The Canadian gave the impression that he understood all the political nuances in the country; and in fact did say that he had heard the Minister speak at the meeting in question. "They think they could handle me?" The lady sitting in the chair beside him patted him gently, like a mother patting a child who had achieved some new facility. "They had some yardfowls up there. Come trying to heckle me. Heckle *me*? Wait, they think I is the Prime Minister that they could heckle? Heckle *me*? One fellow then had the guts to ask me what happen to Pond. What happen to Pond? He think he had me in tights. But he don't really know me. Pond? 'Pond,' I said, 'Bo, Pond didn't tell me his business, so I can't stannup 'pon a flatform in front o' these people, and tell you nothing 'bout Pond.'"

"You handled that question like a diplomat," the Canadian representative said. "It could have been a ticklish situation for the government. As you know, the cabinet hasn't declared its position on that one yet. Not so far as I've been able to gather."

The Minister now turned all his attention to the Canadian. He anticipated that the Canadian might be about to reveal too much knowledge of the confidential workings of the government; and even though they were all friends in this expatriate's house, the anxious look that came to the Minister's face said that he had to be careful. He was also aware that there were people present who were not in the government. He glanced anxiously at Shirleigh, and said, "Lemme tell you something, son." The woman beside him was patting him all the while on his back. John Moore could not decide whether it was an approving pat. "I breathe politics. I sleep politics at night. Ask *her!*" He looked back at the lady, whose accommodating smile tightened around her mouth, and her lips formed an O. "When I went up to Oxford University, and sat at the feet of the great George Lowes Dickinson, reading Modern Greats, you think I was up there making sport? And to come back here, to this poor-arse country, pardon my expression, with a lotta yardfowls, and let anyone o' them tie me up? Your-humble-servant? No, son. My old man could hardly afford to send me parcels at Christmas." The lady sitting in the chair pushed him farther away, perhaps to suggest that this time he was going too far.

"I went to the University of Toronto, myself," the Canadian representative said. He was a man with a touch of the ascetic about him. His full-grown beard did nothing to take away his lean look. He was a man who seemed to have been trained, programmed even, to sit in such company and feel relaxed. Perhaps, too, he was a man trained to go to such parties and take mental notes. He seemed to know a lot about the secrets of government and of local politics.

The other Canadian man was a professor on sabbatical, a friend of the representative's. He was writing a
book on local political structures. He said nothing during
the entire conversation. He merely kept his pipe lit, sent
white jets over everybody's head, and nodded when he
approved of a point; and shook his head, as if putting out
the fire in the pipe, when he disagreed with the discourse.
The others just listened to the humor. For it was all
humor. Kwame, the grass-roots politician, had called the
ministers in the government comedians. Shirleigh, for her
own reasons, remained throughout with a cloud of mild
embarrassment on her face. Nobody present took the
Minister seriously, or was impressed by what he had been
saying. It was a joke. The Minister seemed to represent a
group of men with the best brains in the country for chi-
canery, who had banded themselves together and were
carrying on a large joke on the people.

John Moore's mind went back to the debates in
the mock parliament he himself had been a part of
when he was attending Trinity College in Toronto. The
mock parliament used to debate, in traditional and constitutional dignity with wigs and robes, such motions
as, "Be it Resolved by this Honorable House that the
Quality of Dinners on Friday Nights in the Dining Hall
are not Suitable for the Consumption of the Honorable
Scholars in this Ancient Institution." That too was comedy.

When his mind stopped traveling, he heard them
talking about the latest topic in the country: *guns*.

And then he focused, for the first time, on another
guest. A figure who had been sitting in the shadows all
evening. A big man. A very black man. His hair was
clipped very short, like the Minister's, and he had a nervous habit, or an affectation, of bending his fingers and
digging them into his head. He looked like a monkey
when he did this. He carried four or five pencils of differ-

ent models and colors in one top breast pocket; and in the
other was a large black case for his spectacles, which he
would take out, put on, immediately push up on his forehead, and read whatever he intended to read without
actually using them. He had just done this as the Minister
passed something resembling a document over to him.
The man's laugh was the most distinguishing thing about
him. He laughed "Hick-hick!" as if he was coughing. He
was apparently the darling of the group. Everybody
referred to him as the "Chairman."

"Hick-hick!" the Chairman said, handing back the
document, which he refolded in its original creases. "I
agree with you, man!"

"It's about Juliet," the Minister said, laughing.
"Fired his arse, first thing the morning after!" He glanced
in the direction of Shirleigh, who had lowered her head.
"And not one cent in severance pay!"

"Really, he shouldn't have done that," the
Canadian representative said. "And the Prime
Minister's wife present too . . . "

"Johnmoore, boy, I warning you not to tek-him-on
at your place. I hear he came to you asking for a job."

"But you hear the joke he laugh-out at, though?"
the Chairman asked them. Already he was laughing.
"Didya hear, too, who had give the joke? It was a permanent secretary, man, who gave the joke!" He broke down
laughing, and could not, for a while, continue. "The joke
is 'bout a game some little boys used to play, called
'sling-loo!'"

"Jesus Christ, Chairman, yuh can't tell that joke in
here! Ladies and gentlemen present, man!" the Minister
protested.

"Well, it seems as if this game, sling-loo, was
played by some very important people in this country . . .
You see, what you do . . . "

"Chairman!" the Minister shouted.

"Let's hear the joke, man!" the hostess said. It was the first time she had spoken in a long while.

The Chairman started cautiously, "What you do is to put your index finger . . . is it your index finger, or your little finger, Mr. Minister? . . ."

"Jesus Christ, Chairman!"

"Let me get to-hell outta this house!" The voice was so cold, and so high-pitched, that it took John Moore some time before he realized that it was Shirleigh who had spoken her resentment. She was already getting up and heading for the door. "Say it! Say it! Everybody who was born here knows you *stick* your finger in your arse, and then hold it up to the air to see . . ."

" . . . to see if a fly would light on it, and if a fly won't, then . . . " the Chairman went on, mumbling, completely unaware of what had taken place. He was digging his fingers into his brains and his dandruff as he spoke.

Heads turned in one direction, then the other, trying to blame the indiscretion on someone.

"You stupid old bitch!" the Minister said, getting up from the lady who sat beside him, and who remained unruffled in all this. He went out into the other room, where the hostess was trying to comfort Shirleigh. But she had already had enough. John Moore got up and started to go to her. The Minister stopped him, and said, "Wait a minute, Johnmoore, son. She will quiet-down. Let, let . . . ahm . . . " he could not remember his hostess's name, " . . . let her take Shirl outside, and let some fresh air blow in her face. I got to talk to you, son."

It seemed so easy to use one's power in this group; and so easy to settle what had been ruffled. John Moore lingered a while looking back at Shirleigh, as the hostess, as if the suggestion of the Minister's had been a command, took Shirleigh through the same door they had entered with such gay expectations.

The Canadian representative sat back down. Everybody sat back down. There was some strange protocol in operation; and at the same time, it seemed as if even those who had been injured by it could not exert their equality in the face of this protocol.

The Minister put his arm round John Moore's shoulder and said, "We are planning something big, something important for this country, and I want your support." John Moore nodded, not intending commitment, but out of laziness to speak. He was too upset. "Good. Now we having some meetings soon. I will get back to you." The Minister had a way with people: he patted John Moore on his back, and smiled, and said, "Wait, what happen in here? Somebody dead? Man, let we drink some real liquor now!" The Canadian representative got up. The Canadian professor got up. The Chairman got up. John Moore was still standing. All these men, except the American, formed themselves into a group, like men, like men in this part of the huddling powerful world, and drank, and laughed, and told the joke of sling-loo, where discretion, propriety and even protocol had no place. After all, the protocol was their own creation. The Minister recaptured some of his previous style when the talk got back to guns in the country.

"Somebody foolish enough to bring guns in a country where I is a cabinet minister? And me, Your-humble-servant living here? There is too many grass-roots politicians running 'bout this place. They all want locking-up. Give them to me, man! I will lock them up. If the Prime Minister frighten to lock them up, Your-humble-servant would turn the key 'pon them. If I was attorney general, you think they would *dare*? *I* told them yardfowls the other night 'pon that flatform, *'Don't ask Your-humble-servant 'bout Pond; don't come to me with that foolishness. Pond borrow money and didn' remember to pay it back. He even borrow a million dollars from the Cubans.*

Don't ask me for Pond, man.'" The men, circumscribed in this circle, laughed. "This country need a revolution, if yuh ask me. There's a time for reaping and a time for planting. I didn' say so. The poets say so. And that particular poet is in the Bible, the greatest book in the whole damn world, son. The greatest, and with the prettiest language, son."

"Pond borrowed one hundred thousand from us, too," the Canadian representative said.

There was stunned silence. The circle was almost about to break up. Hands fell, slowly, off shoulders.

"The Lord giveth, and the Lord taketh away," the Chairman said, after some time had elapsed. But his words had no meaning now. Something had happened already.

The Canadian representative said he was getting tired. "Some people from the Other party coming to see us at nine."

"Don't give them one blind cent!" the Minister cautioned him. "Not cent-one!"

"The leader and the deputy-leader."

"I wish they were coming to *me!*" the Minister said. And no one needed to know what he would do with them. The circle formed again, stronger than before; and in its confines, they each fired another straight scotch.

A plane was coming in to land. They had already forgotten about planes. They had eaten too much and drunk too much. Nobody bothered to say whether the plane belonged to BWIA or Pan-Am. It was just a plane. It was left there, suspended like most things with which they had to deal, hanging there, undisputed and unsettled. Planes had tickled their curiosity earlier in the night. Now, no one in this new circle cared a damn. They were filled with drink and with food. And with power.

Shirleigh came back with the hostess. They seemed to have become closer during their walk in the garden.

"Ready?" she said to John Moore.

"A toothache coming on, so I had better turn-in, too," the Chairman said.

"Johnmoore, boy!" the Minister said, smiling. "We have plans. Don't forget." He walked up to Shirleigh, put his arm round her shoulder, and kissed her. Before he even moved away, she passed her hand lightly over her cheek where he had planted the kiss. It was the only protest she seemed able and perhaps powerful enough to express.

The black woman appeared again. He could see the great black strength in her breasts. They were covered in a white halter top; but he could still see the large black inner circles beneath the white sheer. Her eyes were large and beautiful, and they were filled with water . . .

John Moore glanced through the morning newspaper on his desk, and turning to the inside pages, saw this story: *"Ebenezer Jones, 23, of Wright's Village in the city, was yesterday sentenced to five months in prison for stealing $50 (Canadian) from a tourist from Toronto, Ontario, Canada. Jones was accused of entering the tourist's room in a west coast hotel. The young Canadian lady was attending the hotel's weekly barbecue and dance. Judge J. O. K. Evelyn said, in passing sentence on Jones, that 'the criminal element in this country must be stamped out without trace. This country lives off the economic avails of tourism. Many well-meaning tourists come to our shores for peace and rest and hospitality. This country is known the world over as a hospitable place. I shall not tolerate, and indeed the judicial system of this country cannot tolerate, such criminal and embarrassing delinquency.' Jones's sentence is to be with hard labor. He had no previous criminal record. Jones is what is known locally as a 'beach boy,' a breed of young boys who are plaguing the tourist industry of the country."*

Weekesie called soon after to ask him if he had heard about Juliet Harris. All ministries, he said, had been asked not to offer Julie any employment.

"You see what I was telling you about this system?" he asked, unnecessarily. "Just as I said, the Rev was the man who told the Prime Minister."

"It's hard to believe, though."

"How are you going in the job? Don't forget that I promised to show you some pictures. What about coming around next weekend for drinks, eh?"

"I'll see. I am working on a paper for the minister in charge of culture, something to do with national culture. Priority, as he said, when he called yesterday."

"Look, man. Let me give you some advice. There is no such word in the civil service of this country. Or in other countries. Ministers always use that word, but it doesn't mean that they are going to read and study the damn paper when you write it."

"This is important, though. And I should do it."

"I am not telling you not to do it, you blasted fool," Weekesie said. "I just telling you don't run your blood to water before the weekend. You have some nice sexy pictures to censor . . . after all, you's the big man in culture these days . . . "

Soon after the article about Ebenezer Jones appeared, the leading calypsonian, Lord Leadpipe, wrote a song about it, in which he said:

> *Tell the governor of the Central Bank*
> *That a new rate o' exchange floating-'bout,*
> *Ebenezer borrow fifty dollars to feed he mout'*
> *And for every ten, Jones get a mont' in the tank!*

It soon became a popular song, and made the top ten on the hit parade on GBS. People sang it and danced to it at parties. It was becoming a kind of signature for one particular disc jockey on GBS. The orchestration of the calypso contained sound effects of waves and guns throughout the chorus. There were other sound effects of breaking glass and the firing of revolvers. The grass-roots section of the population loved the calypso, and embraced it as their own ideology. And wherever you went in the city, on Saturday mornings in particular, you would see large numbers of young men standing idle beside the doors of shops where the tourists bought duty-free goods; and these young men would be watching them, and would hum the chorus, and make the sound effects of breaking glass and guns and waves, hissing the chorus through their clenched teeth. Soon, the Board of Tourism received reports that the tourists were becoming too nervous to shop in the city. Businessmen complained that the calypso was causing them to lose trade. The boys at the doors on Saturday mornings loved the reaction to Ebenezer Jones's song. That was what they called it: not "The Rate of Exchange," as Lord Leadpipe christened it, but "Ebenezer's song." As a beach boy, Ebenezer used to spend all day, every day of the week, on the beaches of the popular tourist hotels; just sitting and waiting. He would sit a few feet away from the tourists who lay in the lounge chairs tanning themselves. And he would not have to sit too long, not for more than an hour, before a tourist, woman or man, would come up to him and pretend in the foreplay of this well-established bargaining for an acceptable rate of exchange, body for bread; and end up by taking Ebenezer into the hotel room, and putting him into bed, for twenty Canadian dollar bills. There was similar trade with Americans in American dollars. The Saturday-morning boys said that was the price of one orgasm. And twenty more for each succeeding "discharge." "Them tourisses hungry as shite, man," the Saturday morning boys would say, as they hummed Ebenezer's song. It was his tune. It talked about his way of life, and, of course, theirs too. All his friends knew of Ebenezer's sexual prowess. And lots of Canadians and Americans, men and women, thought "what a fine boy" Ebenezer was. Before he was twenty-one he had already made ten first-class airplane flights to Canada and the United States, on the invitation of these ladies and gentlemen who did not intend to forget easily the satisfaction he had given them during their seven or fourteen days sunning themselves on the beautiful beaches of his beautiful paradise of a country.

And then a strange thing happened. Ebenezer got greedy. And a little pompous, and perhaps tired from the exhausting organ-grinding. And he stole money. From the same young woman who had paid him twenty dollars the night before for his body. The court reporter did not know these facts: they were known only to Ebenezer's friends and his lawyer, who refused to use them as extenuating circumstances.

Another strange thing happened. The week after Ebenezer had been in prison for one month, GBS presented a press conference called by the minister of tourism. The businessmen and hotel owners and managers and the tourists themselves were nervous. At this press conference the national anthem was played. And on this day, the whole country was listening. By artistic coincidence, the first ten bars of the calypso were almost identical to those of the national anthem, but sung at a different tempo. Lord Leadpipe had an uncanny sense of national humor. At the end of the minister's press conference, there remained about three minutes of air time to fill in; and the operator on duty, a very fat brown-skinned man, pressed a button and the verse of "The Rate of Exchange" dealing with the rate of exchange was played to the entire, open-mouthed, ecstatic nation. The minister of tourism was not a popular man.

The next night the minister had to come back on television, and in one sentence said, "The Prime Minister has authorized me to inform you that the calypso entitled 'Rate of Exchange', by the local artiste Lord Leadpipe, is hereby banned from public dissemination on the radio station controlled by this government, and on any of the private radio stations." He had to read the sentence from the script, to make sure, apparently, that he was following the letter of the law. A new law was passed about the national anthem and the national flag; although no one in the country who sang the calypso understood what the relationship was between flag and national anthem. But the government had spoken. And the minister had spoken on behalf of the Prime Minister.

"When the government say so, is so, man," the woman said, and then laughed. They were having lunch that afternoon at one of the hotels. "The Lord giveth, and the Lord taketh away."

Lord Leadpipe was interviewed on television and radio soon after the minister's second appearance, and when asked what he intended to do about the banning of his hit tune, he said, "I working on the music of another one, called 'The Lord Giveth!'" The interviewer broke into unabashed laughter, and almost spoiled the entire program. Rumors began to spread. People were saying "Brek-for-yourself!" and knowing what it meant. Talk spread. It was said that the manager of GBS had been fired; that the interviewer, the announcer of the first press conference, the assistant program manager of radio and the assistant program manager of television had been fired. Talk spread that the Director of National Culture had been ordered by the minister to monitor all the cultural programs planned for GBS. Panic was everywhere. And the brush would sweep clean. People in power, John Moore knew clearly, were tough. They acted tough. But the ordinary people continued to sing Ebenezer's song at the doors of the dutyfree shops in the city on Saturday mornings. And if one listened carefully, one could hear snatches of the song on the very beaches where it had had its origin, as the tourists lay in the sun, skinned and burned, or under umbrellas, drinking rum punches with nutmeg in them, eyes on the native boys.

Kwame, the grass-roots politician, held a mass meeting and talked about the calypso; and said, "This government is a unjust government. Do you know that this government have just fired twenty employees of the Government Broadcasting Service? And for what? For playing a damn calypso!" The audience bawled. Kwame then dealt with the minister responsible for broadcasting and culture, and told the people, "And that man wasn' even rass-hole borned here!" The newspapers took up the matter, letters to the editor filled both papers, and the Ministry of Tourism was obliged to act again. It conceived a carefully designed plan to counteract the nationalism in the country: a yearly festival to be called CRAPPO. A ministry press release disseminated throughout the country, and in all media, said that the acronym stood for the "Cultural Regeneration of the Arts of the Peoples' Pragmatic Orientation." The minister said that the Prime Minister had directed him to put aside one million dollars to make this festival "a national indigenous success." The Director of National Culture was not consulted in any of these preparations. It was he who had thought that "The Rate of Exchange" was culturally relevant to the consciousness of the grass roots; and had worked behind the scenes to get the calypso played as often as possible. He was isolated. He was ignored. Preparations and plans had been authorized without his being asked to take part. So, he remained silent. He really did not know what to do. He had thought of asking the minister responsible for a meeting. But he was not sure.

"Don't do that," the woman said. "That's not what you should do. You know what you should do? Nothing."

"But I am the Director of National Culture!"
"They know that."
"What should I do then?"
"Let's make love."

His only solace now was the beach. He would go there often, always with the woman, because he did not wish to be mistaken for a beach boy. But in some tempting moments, he would think seriously of becoming a beach boy. He might learn, first hand, something about the particular sexual nuances of his country. Weekesie had been complaining that he would not visit him, as he had promised, to look at the photographs. "These photos, old man," Weekesie had said, disappointed by postponement of the appointment, "these photographs would give you a hard-on! I took them myself. In one of my apartments that I rent-out to the tourists. So I ought to know their genuine hard-on value, man!" Weekesie had been drinking, heavily. And he seemed to sober up when he added, "But in confidence, buddy, nobody is to know that I am the photographer."

Many ministers owned apartment-hotels which they rented only to tourists, in foreign currency; and some of them went into business with private citizens who trafficked in the tourist women. A lot of money was made in this business.

But the tourist women brought with them a certain rough-hewn principle of fair play and racial democracy, which was not previously known in the country. These women slept with whom they wished. They talked with whom they wished. They walked the streets, wearing bikinis, with whom they wished. And they spent their money, and quite a lot, on whom they wished. The Ministry of Tourism contemplated writing a code of tourist ethics. John Moore had heard confidentially, from Weekesie, that the minister, once a tourist from Australia before he became a naturalized citizen of the country, had drafted the code himself. He was worried, Weekesie said, about *"the phenomenal number of visitors to our country who miscegenate with a certain class of native men."* Weekesie cautioned him not to repeat it, because it was a direct quote from the preamble to the code.

His only solace nowadays was the beach, where he would go with the woman in the late afternoon. They were there now, and preparing to go into the water. She tested the coldness of the waves; and gave off a light-hearted shriek. "I notice something about you. You don't venture near the sea save I standing next to you. That mean you love me so much, or you 'fraid somebody mistake you for a beach boy?" And when she laughed at her own lightheartedness, the space between her teeth showed wider, and more enticing. She made him see through some of the things she said that she was still in touch with the native heartbeat of gossip and talk. "My roots," she called it. Through an accident or a slip in something she had told him, he found out that she had been hearing a lot of things said about him. "And I find myself — I don't know — always taking your side. I didn't take Julie's side, imagine that. And in a way, he is closer to me than you could ever be, at least for the moment. Julie gave me three children. But here I am, twenty years removed from the first time I told you no in no uncertain terms, now begging you to let me tell you yes. Life is a bitch, isn't it?" But she had so far not told him precisely what was being said about him. "They call you a radical, sometimes," she had told him once.

All in all, knowing these things about himself did not make him any more secure about his residence in the country, and about his return; and the earlier feeling of confusion soon degenerated into paranoia. He had never before in his entire life felt so unsafe.

He had felt it the first night he heard Kwame exhorting the people at the political meeting. Kwame had frightened him. There was too much violence in his language. That violence had slipped over in everyday usage, too. Bus conductors were violent to passengers, and hawkers in the markets were violent in this same oracular way to the people who bought from them. He had kept this feeling from the woman. He couldn't expose himself to her. For she might conclude that he had become much too North American. That night when they had got out of the car to listen to Kwame speak, he rationalized that he did it because he wanted to know the pulse of the country. In this, he was no differently patronizing than the Canadian professor on sabbatical, intent upon writing a book on the political structures of the country in one year. He wanted to know the pulse of the people. Everybody had been talking to him about the tension in the country, saying that the people were not happy. That night, as he had gotten out of the car, he had been overcome immediately by the smell of the crowd. And in addition to the smell, there had been this feeling: a feeling of fear. He was, for the first time in twenty years, merely another black man in a crowd of seven hundred black people. He was no longer conspicuous. *One night in 1969 he entered a downtown store to purchase a shirt; and the clerk spent more than ten minutes speaking with someone else at the counter; and hungry and fierce and black and nationalistic in those days, he raised his voice and made a protest like a clarion; and was served almost immediately afterwards, with an apology from the store manager; and weeks later when he had the courage to go back into that store on Yonge Street near Gerrard, the manager came up to him, and made certain that he was served promptly, even before three other white customers who had been in the line twenty minutes before him. He was conspicuous in Toronto.* But here he was just another black man; and no one could tell the difference. No one in that crowd could tell that he was a poet; that he was the new director of their culture. And no one of those seven hundred black people gave a damn. The large crowd had shifted once to accommodate a humorous part of Kwame's speech, and he found himself very close to some man. He could smell that smell on the man. Then he felt a soft sensation under his shoe, and he thought he was stepping on cow manure. The meeting was held in a pasture. He became comfortable to the sensation, and relaxed, and put his weight on both shoes. Suddenly he heard in his ear, like a hiss, *"Tek-yuh-fucking-shoe offa my kissmearse foot, you poor great black stupid son-of-a-bitch!"*

They were sitting at the edge of the water, watching the sea lick their feet. He was glad he had her beside him.

"Years ago, remember, before all these strangers started coming here, we could sit down here all day, in peace, and watch the sun go down. This is the most beautiful time of the day."

It was a cool late afternoon, about six; with the skies blue and clean-looking. It was a tone of blue he had never seen before. The water was blue from the reflection, and the horizon was on fire with the sun sinking to the water. A sailboat was slicing the waves, bound for somewhere to their left. She held up her hand to show him the sailboat. It looked like a folded piece of white paper. She lay back on the sand, and he saw the cut from the surgeon's knife which had gone almost the whole distance from her right side to her left. It awoke the sexual instincts in him. He was sitting with his legs drawn up, and his arms propped around his knees. The sailboat became a larger slice of white paper; and the sun was cut in half by the edge of the water in the colored distance. All of a sudden, there was a roar of a boat. Behind the boat was a woman water-skiing. Until they went out of sight there was no more sun, there was no more peace, there was no more quiet. Only the ugly white wave behind the noisy boat and behind the skier. The skier was close enough for them to see that her exposure to the sun had been sudden and reckless, and that her body was as red as a lobster's. And as the noise faded, the sun almost gone, the peace came back and the beach was quiet, and the woman sat upright and dragged herself close, very close to him, sitting now on wet sand because a wave had come up while they were watching the skier. A white crab, almost completely transparent, was running away from the wave. The woman rested her head on his shoulder, and he felt for the first time what she meant when she said that this time of the day was the most beautiful. It corresponded with a deep surging feeling of beautiful lust within his body.

The sun went down. The sea out beyond where they could see was like a volcano's mouth, gasping fire; and the sea was like a fan whose ribs were painted in colors which neither of them could name. Behind them were the trees, and a bar where tourists were drinking. There were Manchneedle trees, which look like fruit trees, and beach-grape trees which never bore fruit long enough to be tasted because of the boys who scavenged the beach. And the smell of food cooking for the tourists.

She got up and brushed the sand from her swim-suit, pulled the crease out of the division between her legs, and went into the sea. She bobbed up and down in the warm water, making little splashes, her hair in curled stringy braids, and the water like temporary jewels on her neck. She dived down, and came up beautiful and happy. He watched her, and he knew that he had never seen a full-grown woman laugh and play with such sur-render of body. He thought of the kind of restraint that had kept him in Toronto for those twenty long sidewalk-slipping winters; and he thought of Juliet: why had Juliet renounced all this?

"*Come!*" she screamed, and dived beneath the water. The sun had done the same thing minutes ago. When she came up, she spluttered, "Come. I want you to come."

The blessed woman with her black beauty came running down the beach, bouncing her body with her enticement in his face. He would have to hold her hand some day. But for the moment, she was bouncing her body as if she alone could hear the rhythm of the life and the music that surrounded her. She was the only consolation on this white beach. But she did not know it yet . . .

She had condescended to have a sherry at the tourist bar on the beach. The young barman was wearing the most aggressive Afro hairstyle he had ever seen. The hotel management had clothed its staff in red jackets and red trousers with black frills on the sleeves and parts of the trousers; but this young man had apparently resented such costuming, and had counteracted with his Afro. He carried a small transistor radio around his neck, like a priceless necklace. The hit parade was on. John Moore thought of "The Rate of Exchange." The waiter served them, and stood at the far end of the bar, bored with the music. For a moment, it was quiet. The woman sipped her sherry, and then started to hum a calypso. It took John Moore a while to recognize the tune. The waiter at the far end of the bar came alive, lowered the volume on his transistor, and moved like running water closer to them. She hummed the verse about the rate of exchange. The waiter was almost stunned. He could not under-stand the association of her light-brown complexion, which to him meant something very specific, and the calypso. His face relaxed, and he smiled. Without a request, he brought two more drinks, sherry and scotch on the rocks.

"They could ban Ebenezer's song as much as they like! But there's a lotta Ebenezers in this country," he said. He talked with his back almost turned toward them. He was still not certain that he could trust the woman, and he had not recognized John Moore; at least he gave no notice that he had. "You would have to work in one o' these hotels to see how people like Ebenezer is treated." John Moore prepared to pay for the drinks. The waiter turned the volume up on his transistor, and like water again moved to the far end of the bar.

"Wait! You don't think I know who you is? You isn't Johnmoore the new fellow in culture? Man, them drinks on the house. All o' them. Let the blasted hotel pay for them, man. I hear you is the fellow who pushed Ebenezer's song, man ... "

GBS was playing one of the four daily obituary notices. The organ music which introduced the program was lugubrious. People of a certain class would laugh among themselves at the obituaries on radio; and they would be embarrassed that "we always advertising so much dead-people!" But the program was as natural to the country as the sea that surrounded it. The Reverend Lionel Lipps had called John Moore soon after the incident with the funeral directors to say that "it's a damn pity that some people forget they culture so fast, when they go Away! At any rate, Johnmoore, I've spoken to the Prime Minister about this, and he has told me to get you to apologize to the funeral directors. What the hell, boy! Don't you know that I get paid for funerals? And the larger the merrier!" He laughed as he said this. "No disrespect to the dead, boy, but I work per-capita, not per-diem ... God go with you, boy, and let's get together some Sunday afternoon, at the Rectory ... "

John Moore had said "Fuck you!" to the call. But discretion told him to say it after he had put the receiver on the hook.

"... *Fernandez, better known as 'Cutters,' late of Cats Village, in the parish of Southbridges, father of John, Victor, Dyall and George Fernandez of the same address ...*" the announcer read, with the same mournfulness as the organ in the background. Two other waiters drew closer to the bar to listen. They might catch a name they knew.

"... *and husband of Mrs. Cherrie Clark of Toronto, Monica and Marvo Fernandez of Cats Village ...*"

"I don't know why they don't take those blasted things off the radio!" the woman said.

"Ask the Prime Minister!"

She laughed, and said, "You're getting balls, man, you getting smart. You think the Lord would give you an answer, though?"

"... *permanent secretary in the ministry of agriculture, member of the board of the Industrial and Prices Commission, died earlier this morning. Simpson Taitt Cameron Weekes, the husband of ...*"

"Jesus Christ!"

"I was to see him this weekend ... he had some photographs to show me ..."

"Keep quiet! ... I want to know when the funeral is," she said. The announcer read off that part in the obituary and it seemed that only then could she relax. "I wonder if my black dress need fixing ... boy, that going be a *lovely* funeral!" He had forgotten all these things about the country. A civil servant's funeral was bound to be a large funeral, a "lovely" funeral. She tried not to be preoccupied with the death; but the sherry was now without taste. She had become so sad, and so isolated, like the night when the Minister talked about her ex-husband.

John Moore was stunned by the sudden news of Weekesie's death. He tried to change the subject.

"There's a fellow who works at the culture place by the name of Vagabond, and as far as I understand, he can't leave work any evening unless he steals something. Could be a roll of toilet paper, or a box of staples. Don't you know that one day this son of a bitch came into my office, and proceeded to tell me how to run the place, how to do my job . . . "

"There're a lotta those!"

" . . . Whenever he sees me, he is always bowing, and when he isn't bowing, he is asking for money. 'Skipper, a little something?' But this day . . . don't you know I could have killed the bastard! . . . he is the janitor, and telling me how to run the blasted place! . . . the bastard! . . . 'Sir,' the janitor said, in his usual overweening manner, after he had bowed and saluted, 'Sir, I don't want to tell you how to run your job, but you making a big mistake in dealing with certain people, the likes o' Juliet Harris. Now, I been working here from the time this office open, and I have see directors come and directors go, but if you ask me, you is the first one to give me a fair break. I am at the bottom of the totem pole in regards o' wages and salary, sir, but if you take my advice, with people like Juliet Harris, well, sir . . . I am not telling you how to run your job, don't get that impression offa me! 'Cause you is a intelligent man, as I read in the papers when you get this job. But, sir, you must understand that you is the first colored man to ever seat in that director chair, and I been cleaning that chair for eighteen years now, and never have I seen a colored man occupying it . . . '"

"You mentioned something about Weekes and photographs, didn't you?" she said. "There was some talk before you came back 'bout photographs and certain people . . . " And the thought faded as unexpectedly as it had come.

"One day, this same Vagabond and another staff member, thinking that I was out of the office, because the door was left open, were talking. Christ, you should have heard what they said about me!"

"Did you say that Weekes promised you some pictures?"

"To show me."

"Did you?"

"I'll never see those pictures now."

"I'm going to find out 'bout those pictures. Something's worrying me 'bout this. Dead too quick, boy . . . he was at the same party as me, two nights ago. He died too sudden . . . "

"Vagabond and this other fellow, a driver for the office, were talking. 'How you like working for that man, Johnmoore, though?'

'For him? You mean with him! Who the hell he think he is? Because he live up in Canada, he think he could come down here and order people all 'bout the place!'

'He good, though?'

'Good, shite!'

'But they say he used to teach at a lotta universities in Europe and the States, and that . . . '

'Powerful, shite! I tell the Prime Minister about he, though! Powerful? Man, be-Jesus Christ, Johnmoore is only a colored boy that uses to live across the road, over there, man. He is only a colored man! No colored man can't be so powerful in this country, man.'

'Wait! You prefer the fellow who uses to smoke the pipe and didn't say nothing all day long, to Johnmoore?'

'Now, that was a gentleman! I did like working for him. He would drop a dollar-bill in my hand now and then. I don't believe in having no colored man over me, as no director. This director-job shouldda been given to another white man.'"

"I wonder if my black dress, ready . . ."

"Are you listening?" She nodded; but she hadn't heard a word about Vagabond. "Vagabond laughed then, and said, 'Man, me and the Prime Minister was talking 'bout Johnmoore, and the Prime Minister tell me that that colored man who does sit-down in that director chair, be-Christ, the Prime Minister say he ain't sitting-down long in that chair. Mark my words! You shouldda hear what the Prime Minister said concerning colored people in big chairs!'"

"He's talking the truth, though."

"Who?"

"Vagabond. The Prime Minister has that habit o' listening . . ."

He was a man about five feet ten or eleven inches. Perhaps he was six feet. And you would readily agree that that was tall if it were not for the shape of his body. He walked like a man who was drunk. But you knew, because of his leading position, he could not be drunk that often. He walked like a seal. From side to side. If you could ever catch him looking at you, looking into your eyes, which he did very seldom, you could see the large eyeballs and the red in them, probably, you would tell yourself, from the amount of hard work which he had to read every night, as the people said, or from drinking. But you would have remembered that he could not, in his leadership position, be a constant drinking man, although drinking was, next to infidelity, the national pastime. His hair was always cut short; but in recent times, with the fashion of Afros among the radical students at the university, whom he did not like — the university and the students, that is — he had started to grow long sideburns. He always carried a comb and a small brush in his soft black leather briefcase. He was a man of about fifty-five years, but he wanted to be much younger, and he wanted to look much younger. And he did certain things which younger men would do. He would leave his office at about five o'clock each evening, and make the rounds of women he kept. There was a local woman who was black. There was one who lived in a South American country during weekdays, but who would fly home, like a called pigeon, for the weekends. There was a European woman. But this European woman — you couldn't tell her nationality, precisely. She might have been German, judging from her accent, and from the recent popularity of German tourists who the minister responsible said were good dollars for the country, and who drank local beer, and then banked on their superiority that they could call the natives "natives," and get away with it; they said that he liked European women best of all his women. They said that he preferred white people to black people. Younger men whom he used as chauffeurs began to laugh at him and at his prowess, but he was a man who they said had power. In this country, they said, a man's power was in his penis. In this country a man's power, not his prowess in anything, was beginning to be measured by the number of women he had. And this man had five, or six . . . depending upon where you counted. But don't let nobody fool you; a man with all that weight to carry around in his black leather briefcase, and with all that age, can't be no kiss-me-arse gorilliphant in bed, unless he is sleeping. The young men he had around him used to laugh at him behind his back and help him out with his prowess and his power. And for a while he let them laugh, because he always had a trick with his Afro comb in the black briefcase . . .

"Do you think somebody could've done something to Weekes?" she said. "Yesterday is sudden, too sudden."

"You could be living today, and tomorrow . . . "

"Cut down. That's what it is!" she said. "Cut down. Do you think . . . somebody could have killed him?"

"For what?"

"You know, I've been thinking . . . I've been hear-

things, and now you mentioned those photographs . . .
You know, Johnmoore, it won't surprise me if somebody
poisoned Weekes. It could happen."

"How?"

"It could happen." He was uninterested in her the-
ory, and said so. But this did not prevent her from
speaking her mind. The more she talked about it, the
more feasible it appeared to him; and she spoke about it
not as if it had in fact happened, but as if it were about to
happen. "Drinks. They could put something in his
drink. It happens every day! But all I am going to tell
you is that if ever you are invited to any party, any party
at all, don't you ever put down your glass and walk
away from it! You can never tell who would put something in it, when your back is turned . . . and I'm telling
you this a bit late, even. I watched you put down your
glass at least six times, at that cocktail party where we
met, as you took up your pipe to light it. 'Jesus Christ,' I
said to myself, 'look that careless boy, though!' It was
then that I ran over to save you . . . "

The house in which he lived was a ranch-style, white-painted bungalow, with a fair-sized lawn all around it and a hedge of tropical trees. Vines grew on the roof of the patio, with a collection of dried coconut fronds that really formed the roof. The lawn always needed cutting. A "piece-time" gardener who worked in the neighborhood asked fifty dollars "to clean-up the place," so he would have to cut the lawn himself. He tried to follow the example of a very buxom, sensual-looking housewife who cut hers with a machete; but he found out she had been born in Trinidad, of Indian parents, and so he gave up on that idea. So far, none of the neighbors had come to welcome him.

The neighbor on his right was what they called an "expatriate;" John Moore sometimes saw him while being served breakfast by his maid on the patio. The neighbor on his left was an old black woman who had spent all her young days in Brooklyn where she was born, working in post offices; and who fell in love with the postage stamps which her aunt received on letters "from a distant cousin." She now spent all day under a broad-brimmed straw hat, in a duster, bent almost like a broken L, talking to lettuce, tomatoes and cabbage, which she didn't use at her table, because cabbage gave her too much "gas."

The house John Moore lived in was not a safe house. There had been burglaries in the neighborhood. All the houses in this neighborhood looked like prison cells with the number of wrought-iron bars in their windows and doors. One formerly poor man, the piece-time gardener said, became "a blasted millionaire overnight, selling iron to bitches like these up-in-here!" Many of the houses were rented out at two hundred and thirty dollars a week, in American currency if you please, to tourists who wanted privacy and a swimming pool ("A swimming pool in a country which is really a island, Mr. Moore, and with the best kiss-me-arse beaches in the whole whirrrrl?" the gardener wanted to know); and the services of a maid. The tourist-tenant paid an extra fifty dollars a week, naturally American, for the maid. But the maid was paid eighteen by the owners, in local currency, sometimes twenty in a gesture of benevolence. So the burglars started coming up the hill, with the tourists. Pickings at the hotels had withered after Ebenezer's song became popular. So the house John Moore lived in was not safe. And he could hardly relax in it. The entire neighborhood was not safe.

No one walked on the short streets after seven o'clock. Maids would run across the street to catch the bus at the corner; and each house, except the one in which he lived, had ferocious dogs, which, the gardener said, and cursed as he said it, "are trained to eat-up the blasted black people like me and you, Mr. Johnmoore, who try to make a blasted living in this blasted neighborhood." The dogs on this street did not like pedestrians. The morning after he moved in, he put on his track suit to go jogging. He walked out in the fresh miraculous-bush-tea beautiful morning. He got to the third house, where two black dogs jumped over the wall at him. Back on his patio eating breakfast, he could not help thinking of Sharpsville and Alabama and Montgomery; and about one dog in particular, trained to kill black people, which he had read about in a book called *White Dog*. It was fiction, he said, but the gardener disagreed: "Let me tell you something, Mr. Johnmoore, that you won't know. Is this. A dog from up in these parts never jump 'pon a white man, except to kiss him. Don't laugh, Mr. Johnmoore. I talking from observance. You see, Mr.

Johnmoore, when a black person sees a dog, because of a number of things which I don't particularly understand, that black person will, first thing, start running. Or think first of running. After many times, sir, that dog get to know the reaction in black people. Don't laugh, I talking from observances, Mr. Johnmoore. Well, if you is a man, walk out there in that road, then! . . . "

White Dog.

That afternoon, when the gardener told him his "observances" about dogs, he got up from drinking with him and went into his study to look for *White Dog.* But the book was not there. It had been left in Toronto. He called some of his friends, but none of them had heard of *White Dog.* Nobody in this country read books sufficiently to have come across it. He *must* get his books shipped here as soon as possible.

He was in this same study now. It was about nine o'clock at night; and he was trying to work on some poems which had been circulating in his head for some time now. The words were there, but they came on to the paper only as words.

He got up and went into the master bedroom. He lay aslant the bed, to think about the poem. He thought about Weekesie. And he started to worry about poisons and pictures and photographs important enough to have a man killed for them: important enough to be put into the poems; and to think of *White Dog* of which the gardener had brought back the memory . . . to think of the loneliness in this beautiful land. To think of the beautiful green land, where all the successful people he had met bragged to him about their dual citizenship, "America and here," or "Canada and here." To think of the woman who had been so attentive. What was he going to do with her? To think . . .

The poem became even more confused in his mind. And he started to dream of Toronto: *he is there and it is early January and it is cold and the snow is falling heavily and he is in bed in a warm house and outside the night is white and cold, and all of a sudden the coldness penetrates the warm house and soaks into his body and he feels he is going down deep into a snowbank being sucked into a lake which has become ice; and he feels an uncomfortable wetness like in a dream that is wet or like when he used to wet his bed and his clothes were cold at first and then warm.* And he jumped up.

Just as he looked, there was a face moving from the louvers. At least he thought so. The water was pouring in straight at him, like connected white bullets. Someone had put the hose, opened at full blast, through the louvers. And had aimed it right at his head. He was looking into the muzzle of the cock. The room was dripping wet, as were his clothes in the cupboard, where the jet of water had moved when the person ran off. And then he could hear a hissing sound of water outside on the oil drums cut in half to hold the half-dead zinnias.

He caught himself, after some effort, and ran out of the house. Going round in the back where the hose was, he lashed his face on the thorns in the uncut bushes there. He must remember to ask the gardener . . .

He turned off the water. And it alarmed him when he could not hear the splashing inside the master bedroom anymore. The louvers were open. He could see the bedroom in water, the bed swimming in water, all his clothes dripping wet.

He could feel someone in the backyard with him. Someone was there watching him. He became even more frightened. And he ran back into the house and locked the door. He checked the other doors, the front door and the door to the patio that led to the green vines and the dried coconut fronds. And then he closed all the louvers. Inside the master bedroom, standing in a pool of water, like a child foolish in his own unwanted pee, he thought of someone to call. If only his neighbors had been neighbors, he might ask them to help him look. But he did not know their telephone numbers. He thought of calling the woman. But he hesitated: could she herself have done this thing, as a prank?

It could have been a gun. Suppose it had been . . .

Sinus-dripping came on during the night, as he sat numbed with fatigue and fear in the airless house. Each time a car slowed down, he peered frightened through a cracked louver, and in this way, he stayed with the night. Just before fatigue took complete possession of him, the telephone jarred him awake. It was the woman.

"*Just what I told you!* A doctor-friend just called me . . . Somebody put something in Weekes's glass, just what I said! You go back now, and finish your rest . . . "

And it turned into dawn with relief; and he was outside bending down searching for footprints. Rain had fallen during the night.

"Well well well! I never knew you were an early riser. *Good* morning, Mr. Moore. Nice morning isn't it? *This*, my brother, is what the tourists pay like hell for. But we have it for *free*, every blessed day that the Lord sends. And by the way, Mr. Moore, if you don't mind me saying it, don't you think a man could hide in your grass, it so tall all round your house? . . . You *should* do something about it . . . "

The Reverend Lionel Lipps was there. John Moore was surprised to see that the Chairman had been invited too. It was the meeting mentioned to him some time ago by the Minister who called himself "Your-humble-servant." Kwame, the grass-roots politician, was there. John Moore didn't know that Kwame was supporting the government these days.

"So this is the young bright prodigal son!" he greeted John Moore. He looked as if age could never touch him physically. "Brother, you stood-up like a man on that Ebenezer calypso-thing. Principle! *Them* don't know 'bout that! The worst thing in the whirl was for the Prime Minister to put a foreigner-man as minister o' culture."

John Moore saw the danger in answering. This had been Weekesie's problem. He would never become so sloppy and fat with a belly like Weekesie and most of the politicians. But this country he loved so much, with its land and its possibilities, was preventing him from thinking clearly, from concentrating, from creating. All he was now hearing around him was talk. *Talk.*

"You didn' say nothing you shouldn' say," Kwame was telling him. "It's a matter o' common knowledge that none o' the ministers in the government like the Prime Minister, 'cause they're always plotting to overthrow him. You can say I say so."

John Moore looked around to see who had heard. The host was at the far end of the verandah of the beach house where the meeting was being held, talking excitedly to the Minister.

"Sit down, gentlemen," he said. John Moore had never met this man before; but he knew from the newspapers that he too was a cabinet minister. He was a silent man. And if his silence was not a cover for his dumb-wittedness, he nevertheless had a reputation in the country for being silent, snobbish and dumb-witted. But he had degrees from two universities; and his father had given him this beach house, where he met his constituents every Sunday morning between seven and eleven. They said that he entertained "better people" in his large home in a place called The Gardens.

The men moved their beach chairs into a semicircle.

"Let's begin, gentlemen," the host said. "I think the Minister would like the floor." He then immediately looked as if he was dozing, the large eyes and the slightly protruding bottom lip giving that impression, and he folded his hands and placed them on his belly. He looked like a silent concertina.

"Fine!" the Minister said. "Lemme tell you fellows something. We ain' here tonight to make sport. Something damn serious happening in this country." All the men knodded, knowingly. "There's three hundred mercenaries here. I for one isn't going to sit back and let them snatch the country outta our hands, so what we have to do is this. In plain language, we have . . . to stir up . . . some violence in this country . . . to counteract those mercenaries, of course! You understand the tactic?" The host had not even opened his eyes at the mention of violence. A fly lighted on his bottom lip. "You-all know what violence mean. A lotta innocent people going get hurt, but there is means and ends in every crisis." He took a paper from his pocket, unfolded it, and said, "This paper is dynamite. Confidential. I get it from a friend o' mine in the Canadian High Commission." He cleared his throat and read:

"One. Considerable arms and ammunition are now stockpiled in the country. Three hundred mercenaries are now in the country, equipped with modern automatic weapons. Two . . . " and he paused. John Moore, growing more uncomfortable, looked up and saw that the other men were holding their heads down. "Two. High Commission information sources suggest that the security forces of the country are inadequate to contain this terrorist group. There is no similar physical destructive potentiality on the government's side. Three. At least three foreign governments with diplomatic representation in the country are in collusion, both with money and with materials, supporting this terrorist group. Four. Core-group heading this terrorist group of mercenaries is comprised of three members of the Other party and one high-ranking representative of the government, a minister. Five. Members of the business community in the country, and some from the private sector, are giving moral, financial and tacit support to this terrorist organization . . . " He folded the paper, put it back into his pocket, and said, "There's more. But you get the picture."

The Chairman started to cough, "Hick-hick!" The sea was at rest and the crickets were chirping. John Moore thought of *White Dog*, and of asking the woman if she had ever heard of a dog like this white dog.

The host was speaking. "We already know the names of this group, and where they hiding the guns," he said. His eyes looked larger and were red.

Kwame, feeling he had to say something, said, "Man, this ammunition was discussed at the last cabinet. I know that." No one seemed worried that he had this confidential information. But suppose it was not really confidential information!

"That is true," the Minister said, conceding that there was such a discussion. He seemed to do it reluctantly, however. "Tonight, though, we meeting to form a *hoonta*. For security reasons we'll call it only *hoonta*. Now, there ain' going be any notes and no minutes, and nobody who's here tonight don't know anybody else who's here. They got some people in this community who think I forgot how to think. But Your-humble-servant didn' go up to Oxford for nothing." The Minister nodded to his colleague; everything was in order; and he continued. "Rev, here, has decided to make a speech in church, around Easter Day. The church will be full o' people, the sermon going be broadcast island-wide, and that will give us a ready-made audience."

"Agreed," Reverend Lionel Lipps said. His pipe was in his mouth, unlit; white hardened saliva on its stem. "Easter Sunday. Resurrection, rising from the dead, and so forth . . . " He seemed to be going over his notes for the sermon in his mind.

"What is the code-name for this operation?" Kwame asked. No one had thought of that; so no one had a ready answer. And no one answered.

The Minister tried to take command of the meeting again. "Now, I letting-go a bomb, now! You are the only people who apart from cabinet will know this." He paused for effect. "*Elections are set for one week after Easter Sunday. This is a secret.*"

On the way to this meeting, the woman, who had driven him, asked him the most incredible question, coming from her. She asked him, "Have you ever seen a dead dog?" When he voiced his shock at the question, she made it more puzzling: "You know when you see a dead dog in the road, sometimes if you are lucky, you will see that dog lying on his back, with all four of his feet sticking up in the air?" It was still a puzzle. "Can't you imagine that, and you are supposed to be a poet?" It was easy to imagine a dead dog in that posture of rigor mortis; but the question itself was the puzzle. People in this country had a most curious way of putting words together. And precisely because he was a poet, it intrigued him: their use of metaphor and imagery. It was the one remaining thing which entranced him, and kept him close to the cultural undercurrent of the country. This way with words. This imagery . . . The Minister was still speaking: "The fellas threw lashes in one another like peas!"

"If I may ask," the Chairman asked, "what exactly is the text going to be?"

"*Anything* but 'The Lord giveth!'" They all broke out into laughter. It went on for some time before the Minister could continue. "That one gone already."

"Jesus Christ!" the Reverend exclaimed. They broke into laughter again.

The meeting then took a more serious turn. "We have the Church organized through the Rev here," the Minister said. "We have to have the Church on our side. And naturally, if everything goes well, Rev will get the hoonta's support for Lord Bishop of the country . . ."

"The Right Reverend, Reverend Lionel Lipps!" the Chairman said.

The Minister knew that he had gone a bit far in offering posts; but he was a clever man.

"Purple-and-gold in your arse! Eh, Rev!" Kwame said, equally impressed.

"I can handle it, man," the Rev said.

"The Church disendow', though!" Kwame added, vindictively. Looks were exchanged: they couldn't be sure where he stood. "The Church disendow', Yuh Lordship."

"Gentlemen," the host pleaded.

"Well, fellas, as to my role. I will make a couple o' speeches in the Market Square, in which I will call for law and order. I is the law-and-order man. But my speech will follow on that of the grass-roots man here, after he already brek-up the place. Well, look, let Karl Marx himself tell you what he will be . . ."

"Who you calling Karl Marx? I am an African scientific socialist, man!"

"Okay, Kwame, okay! Don't lose your head. Two or three speeches on violence, and the country wrap-up in law and order. The police is on our side, too. Hitler ready." There was a chuckle from the Chairman. "Hitler, the commissioner o' police, is a fellow who just *loves* beating-up black power fellows. I met him at a party at the Canadian-fellow place two nights ago, and he tell me personally, that he got his bull-pistle soaking for that occasion. And Hitler say that he looking forward to see the water settle in one o' these black power terrorist's eyes when that first lash land, oh my God!"

"I remember the time," the Chairman began, without asking the chair's indulgence, "I will never forget that day when Hitler lash that beach boy who was terrorizing the tourisses down the east coast, and that first lash brought water to that fellow's eyes; and when the fellow see the water settle in his own eye, he *begged* Hitler to lash him the second time, 'cause that first one had him *bennup*, bent up in two like a hairpin; and the second one straightened him up in truth though, 'cause the first lash really and truly had him mash-up, like a real hairpin. Hitler? Man, Hitler *loves* a piece o' violence!"

Nobody laughed at this anecdote. The host cleared his throat, and took his handkerchief from his pocket, and spat something into it. "Don't you think," he took out his handkerchief again, "that we should," he put it to his mouth, and coughed, "settle on the exact text of the sermon, just in case . . . " He spat a second time into the handkerchief, rolled it, folded it in half, and put it in his pocket again.

"Something from Revelations, I'm thinking of," the Rev said. "It got a sense of Armageddon. It is also relevant. Revelations, chapter 18, verse 21." He cleared his throat. "'*And a mighty angel took up a stone like a great millstone, and cast it into the sea, saying* . . . ' and here is what I consider to be the relevant part, ' . . . *Thus with vio-*

lence shall the great city be thrown down, and shall be found no more.'"

"I don't like the word Babylon. It's a bit too radical."

"Personally, I think that the whole piece is much too violent," the host said. "We shouldn't fight violent acts with violent words."

"What about 'The Lord Giveth,' then?" the Rev conceded.

"I don't like that piece o' scriptures," Kwame said, in a raised voice. "That piece o' scriptures talking too much 'bout the fucking dead! It come from Job. Job, chapter 1, verse 21: ' . . . *and said, naked came I out of my mother's womb, and naked shall I return thither,*' colon, ' . . . *the Lord giveth,*' comma, ' . . . *and the Lord taketh away,*' semicolon, '. . . *blessed be the name of the Lord,*' full-stop!"

"We will use the part with Babylon, then," the Minister said. "That is settled."

Kwame stood up. He had something to say. It was significant that in spite of his inclusion he knew, and the others knew, that he was not their equal. He was the only man present who thought he had to stand to speak. "You asked me here tonight, and I am honored to be included in a move to liberate the people o' this country. Any o' wunnuh in here who hear me speak on a flatforrn, know that I regard the sovereignty of this country as a number-one priority. But before I go on to say that I'm glad that at last there is other politicians interested in this country, and in making the present government more better, let me say this." He was becoming emotional. He was the only speaker who became emotional. "I see that you already promised Rev, here, the Lord Bishopship. I ain't hear nobody promise me nothing. I don't mind that. I am a grassroots man. My motto is, 'He who lives with the grass roots, shall die with the grass roots,' so nobody in here

can't take-away from Kwame *nothing at all,* 'cause
nobody in here haven't given Kwame one blasted thing
yet!" No one made any comment. "Now, so far as this
meeting concerned, I will use the loudspeaking equipment that the attorney general put at my disposal last
year . . . "

"Agreed," the Minister said.

"I don't want anybody to walk 'bout this place
and say that I steal government property . . . "

"Hick-hick!" the Chairman said.

"Won't happen again," the host said.

"Good. Because all I would have to do, is tell the
people the truth. I am in this *hoonter* because I feel it will
do something for the people, the grass roots. Some food
and jobs. I don't know how that going happen, but as
far as I concerned, it should happen in a scientific and
socialistic kind o' way, politically speaking. Otherwise, I
will have to tell the people the truth." And then, satisfied that he wouldn't have to tell the people the truth, he
sat down.

"Agreed," the Minister said.

"The next meeting you will be told about," the
host said. "This one was just to see how the wind blowing . . . "

"Also, in what way we can get Johnmoore here to
contribute," the Minister said. It did not sound so much
like an afterthought as it sounded very dangerous.

"They probably want to talk to you about running
in the coming elections," the woman had said, driving
him to the meeting. He had not been able to imagine a
dead dog to her satisfaction. "The *Weekly*, as you know,
wrote something about your being a candidate. But that
is all lies." She was less interested in that kind of politics
than he was. "Don't be afraid. Go. It may be a good
experience for you." He was not even interested in having the kind of experience she talked about. Just before

they reached the beach house, she had asked him again, "Have you imagined yet what a dead dog would look like?" He wanted to be somewhere else . . . but the Minister was beside him, with his hand on his shoulder.

"Good *boy!*" he said. "Get yourself a drink, and let's talk."

"*Good* boy!" the Chairman said, and then moved away.

"Let we sit down, son, over here." They were alone at the far corner of the veranda. The tourists in the hotel next door were laughing and dancing, becoming boisterous and happy. A steel band orchestra was playing Ebenezer's song. John Moore wished he could be a tourist, and enjoy the country . . .

"Don't listen to that tribal music, son."

"I think it's a good tune."

"Anyhow. Some weeks ago, my colleague in culture announce something about a national cultural festival, CRAPPO, and things like that. You know what I talking about?"

"I think so."

"Good. Well, I want you to write a paper to point out that that is a damn lotta foolishness. But you got to be careful in pointing out, in your paper, that such a festival would cost the taxpayers not ten thousand which is the cabinet figure, but *one hundred* thousand, which is my figure. Taxpayers' money, son. Taxpayers is voters. Voters keep me as a minister. Understand? That is politics . . . "

"How long a paper?" John Moore asked, for no conceivable reason. He knew he wasn't going to write the paper; and he knew that, according to Weekesie, the Minister would forget about the paper, and would never ask for it. But you had to give them the impression, Weekesie said, that you were interested in them. "How many pages?"

The Minister felt in his shirt pocket, and took out the same document from which he had read earlier. He unfolded it, and started to count its pages. John Moore was speechless. The "document" was four pages long. The top page contained five lines: *"Now is the time for all good men to come to the aid of the party"* repeated five times. He saw John Moore looking at this page, and he placed it at the bottom, and so forth until he had exhausted the document. The other three pages were filled from top to bottom with "Now is the time for all good men to come to the aid of the party." Someone had been practising the touch of a typewriter.

John Moore remembered that when the Minister had started to read the document, which he said came from Canadians, all the others were holding their heads down; and the host, who was sitting on the Minister's right, was dozing.

"*Now* you know how much I'm depending on you." There were so many meanings that could be read into the nuances of his language that John Moore was not sure whether the Minister was aware that he had seen the typewritten practices on the document.

He saw the black blessed flesh on this woman's hips. The hips drew his attention to her face and eyes and long nose and deep forehead. He would call her, from now on, Nefertiti. For she was the most wholesome being in the country . . . Nefertiti . . .

Going to her place, for the first time, he was silent. She was doing all the talking, and it helped keep him from thinking of the dangers in his involvement with the "hoonta."

"All you need is a little pill. I think you can buy one from any drugstore, but I'm not sure," she was saying. "Drop it in a person's glass, and that's it, bingo! There is a concentrated tug on the bowels or the intestines and the pain is severe, and such that the person thinks he's suffering from a bad bout of gas in the stomach. People in that situation would run to the bathroom with a bottle of Eno's, you know? Or Epsom Salts. But none o' them two would help them." He had developed the habit, recently, of sitting through the most involved conversation, or speech, and letting the words hit his ears and fall off. He was good at it. But he had missed many important things. How many of the things she had told him had he missed? He knew he hadn't missed much from the conversations of his superiors; for they only talked about their sexual prowess. "Just a little pill," he caught her voice, rambling on. "Or it could be in the form of dust. And the victim would wriggle-up on the floor, or in the bathroom. Like a slug with salt on it. Get smaller, and smaller. Like a worm. Like something that ages all of a sudden. Wrinkled and old. That is," she said, coming to the end of her discourse on poisons, "one consequence of a social murder. I told you to be careful."

Traveling in her car this Sunday evening, he had lots of time to think about his dreams. His dreams were no different from those of the Reverend Lionel Lipps, but the Reverend seemed to be inordinately ambitious; more ambitious than he. The Reverend Lionel Lipps already seemed to have become bishop, on the basis of a word; and before the meeting had ended, he was quoting scriptures to help with the crimson and gold of his aspirations: "This is a true saying, if a man desire the office of bishop, he desireth a good work;" and the grass-roots politician, Kwame, had been quick to add, "A bishop then must be blameless, the husband of one wife, vigilant, sober, of good behavior, given to hospitality, apt to teach;" and at this point, quite impressed by their ability to quote scriptures in their individual defense, John Moore had felt that nothing would stop these men, the minister in the government, the minister in the church, and Kwame who ministered to the needs of the poor, from reaching their goals. Perhaps Kwame had the least chance of success.

He had himself actually sat down and thought of becoming a politician, a minister of government; and once he even imagined himself to be the prime minister. But these were the fantasies of distance, when he was far from home. Now that he was home, he thought of those fantasies as seditious; yet there were other real ministers in government who said they would like to be the prime minister; it was a national political joke; and those who did not wish that, argued among themselves about who was the Prime Minister's favorite, the second most powerful man in the country. His own thoughts about being prime minister were enjoyable; what delightful thoughts!

But he could not think, after that, of any policy to give to the people; and he could think of no potatoes and salt fish and jobs for them; his country was so small that you could not find it on some maps of the world; but what the hell had size to do with power? For in this respect he was thinking like a prime minister of a very tiny country; and he liked to be addressed as The Right Honorable, The Right Honorable Johnmoore, and he would make a speech at the United Nations Security Council and take his country officially and diplomatically clean out of the Third World; which World would he then choose? The Fourth! Was there a Fourth World as there was a Seventh Estate? There were more than seven sugar plantation estates in the country; but a prime minister is a man who has the power to choose whichever World is suitable for his country: Fifth, Sixth or Seventh Heaven . . .

They were saying, people who listened to Kwame, that all the prime ministers in this number of the World they had chosen for their country had so many women, "a lotta women" that they could "screw." All those women who liked men who were righteously and rightfully honorable. The rightfully honorable men in this particular numerical World had more power over more women than those black American Honorable Gentlemen of Leisure rightly had. Power. Never mind the prowess. It was the power, Johnmoore. And the glory. Power, another powerful man said, is the best aphrodisiac in the whole world, in any World: First, Second, Third, Fifth . . . think of power . . . all this talk about little ponds; a big frog in a little pond. That was the idle talk of those little frogs in big alien ponds. Whatever happened to Pond? That was the talk of the disenfranchised. As the Rightly Honorable Gentleman of Leisure, PC (Pussy Comptroller of Her Majesty's Layful Governaunce), he would hold everybody's frog in his own hand; and if he wanted a one-party state of group sex, then that would be lawful; and if he wanted to control the masses of mediums in his country, well, fuck it, The Lord Giveth; and if he wanted to be always in their hairs here, and be the Heir and Vice-Marshall of the Hairy Forces of Tourists, like shite, nobody couldn't stop him, and the Lord couldn't tek-it-'way . . .

"Johnmoore, what did you-all talk about so long? I've been trying to get you to talk from the time I picked you up . . . Penny for your thoughts?"

. . . One of the fellows at the meeting had said, "Man, the whole government foops. It is a fooping government!" and they all screamed and collapsed and called one another beach boys and homosexuals; and one fellow had said, "Talk 'bout rumors? Man, you didn' hear that they say I does do it to the Prime Minister, too!" and then there was this silence, and the cards to be dealt in the game were held for a long embarrassed time in the hand of the dealer, and not a man round that table could move or speak, including the "boys" who served drinks and cooked fish and scrambled eggs for the men; because everybody was stung, because the fact was declared.

"Nobody certainly can't say that about you, Johnmoore!"

"What?"

"That you are the most talkative man in the world! . . . Didn't you hear anything I been saying?" He looked out the window, and recognized where he was. "Come inside, man!"

The black beautiful woman had taken off her halter top.

The woman's house has a wall around it. The wall is washed in white. It is almost as tall as you are. And it has spaces, gateways without gates, large enough for her car to come and go through. She gave her house the name "White Gates." You think of *White Dog* . . . Her children have long gone through these same gates. There is an explosion against the white of red flowers running the length of the wall. The wall runs on both sides of the house to the back. Inside the gateways are large white-washed stone flowerpots, patterned after Grecian urns, in which are kept more flowers. These flowers are white. And just beside one large urn on the right, beside the car-port in which she never parks her car, so she boasts, is a thick bush of Lady-of-the-Night. The fragrance is strong and beautiful. You can smell it before you get to her house. The Lady-of-the-Night can do many things to you: if you are happy, if you are in love, it can make love more heady and exciting; and it can make you confuse the smell of the woman, and her armpits with the deodorant that has no smell, with the smell of the flower. And if you are unhappy with a woman, it makes you want to be in her bosom of love, in the thighs, rejoicing at your good fortune, that you have returned to see this strength and smell and godliness in these blessed women of your country, from whom you were so long separated by the miles of your ambitiousness and loneliness. You could not be lonely on a Sunday night here, when the

Lady-of-the-Night bush is giving off this sensual and reminding smell.

Her house is a small tidy house. And at this moment, the most happy corner in the beautiful land.

Her bedroom is small. And it smells of mothballs. There is also the smell of incense, but the mothballs are used, the woman says, to keep her clothes from being eaten up by "these damn moths." There are fragrant soaps, too; but the smell of these cannot out-power the mothballs. But when you are inside the bedroom for some time, the acridness of mothballs disappears; and you are face to face with the flesh of flesh. Honest and clean and with just a hint of perspiration which rewards her hard sixteen hours of honest nurse-work. Then the mothballs disappear after the shower, just taken for your benefit, because she says she is going to screw you to death. You are now washed in a strange smell. The smell of the flowers beside the house, outside the bedroom, which corresponds to the lotion she has used; and the smell of the sea which comes in on you with the gentle breezes that find their way into this bedroom of threats and anticipation. The bedroom becomes a chapel. Once inside it, you have to be true and strong, because people talk; and religious to your intentions. "I going to screw you to death," she has said, more than once. And you find you can't talk too loudly in the orgasm of this delight, just in case, the neighbors . . .

A four-poster is in the bedroom. When you lie in it, upon it, you have to look up into the heavens of your cautious anticipation, and see white silken cloth; you can dream of Henry VIII, that you are he, and you tremble for the soft belly on which you are going to lie. Or you dream of never returning whence you have come, and of forgetting everything. Or you dream about what truth there is in the demanding of women with space between the teeth. And you find yourself lying there, trying to hide the embarrassment of your prowess and confusion and fear for the space between the teeth. And in your worry, you see her let her dress fall, silently like the sea is sometimes, like a challenge upon the floor, and she is dressed only in panties almost the same color as her skin, and that sends pretense and fear into your body; so you hasten from this thinking of your prowess to think of your power in serious important thoughts of the world of politics; and when you find there is no strength, no truth in that, because you are in a chapel now, you wonder what better thoughts could have come into your hesitating intentions, than the thought of her sensual beauty.

There is a slash across her belly. From the practising hand of one of the country's leading surgeons. And you hate the country and the surgeon, in your trembling cautiousness. You notice the first signs of a wrinkled belly. Age, you say to yourself, will help you, creeping into this sepulcher; but sepulchers are mysterious, and you do not know what you will find inside its dark horribleness. You see this body, like the land, which had disturbed you so everlastingly when it was clothed. And now, in its stark enticing nakedness, down to the long years in your groins, you feel a drying-up of water; and you cannot "brek a row."

"Should we turn-off the lights?"

Her voice, too, is not the same as it was in the chattering car. It is a child's voice, a sweet voice, a slightly hoarse voice, a shy voice. A threatening voice. And it confuses you, because whether the lights are turned off, or left burning in their white frosted and patterned shades, what you have in mind to do to this body cannot really be done because of the drought in your groin, and the whole country will hear about it in talk, anyhow. You are ready now to exchange power for prowess. But it is too late now for this change in ambition.

"Is *anything* wrong with you?"

So you continue to look up into the ceiling of this fourposter testing your honesty, and you permit your body to welcome the romantic feeling as your mind wanders on impotency. The woman makes sure that there is music. She puts the music on, in the dining room, on the stereo she keeps there. You think of having no appetite and of sexual appetites, as she turns the lights off. The bedroom is filled now with the music, and outside you can hear nothing. There is nothing else to hear or know. This room is safe and unsafe for you to be in. You can spend the rest of your strength lying here, within the four strong polished mahogany thighs, and not even a prime minister can touch you here. It is more wholesome than a cabinet room. It smells beautiful. The only smell now is the perfume she has used.

"Purple and gold, in your arse, Rev!" Kwame the *grass-roots politician had said, without pretensions.*

There is a thinned-out rim of brown hair around her nipples. Her breasts are firm and they fit into your hands like two well-sized avocado pears. There is the music coming from the dining room. She takes her silken brown scarf off her head and her hair falls reddish-brown on her shoulders, and she shakes it out and it splatters on your face. The Lady-of-the-Night comes through the opened window at the head of the bed, and fills the room. You get up and take off your suit, the shirt-jack which is the official wear of your young, culturally-groping country. On the dressing table is a picture in a white frame of her standing beside a man in a white beard, Juliet. You see yourself and Juliet's reflection in the large mirror on the wall from the floor to the height of your head.

"Come," she says, relieving you of shyness; and her call banishes from you further thoughts of power and prowess and your jealous speculations of Julie's ability to cope with the tumbling belly of this woman, who now becomes like a monster, ready to victimize you . . .

When you lie beside her, you can feel her shudder; and when you hold her strong in your arms, you feel how cold her body is; as if she was exposed too long on the beach after a morning swim. The Lady-of-the-Night comes in. You can feel her anxiety shuddering through her body; and you tighten your grip and squeeze the breasts; and then lower your body down slowly, with the saliva whetting the path of your mouth to her breast, the right breast, and she squirms and shudders and shouts, "Jesus Christ!"

It is all glory for her now, and she knows, she knows, "Oh My God!" that this is the moment she was waiting for . . .

And said, naked came I out of my mother's womb, and naked shall I return thither. The Minister was telling him confidentially, at the beach house, that the minister responsible for culture, "that blasted aborigine," was bringing a national stick-licking competition as part of the CRAPPO Festival, and that he, Johnmoore, must do everything in his power to stop it; and the Reverend Lionel Lipps was rehearsing the text of his elevation: "This is a true saying. If a man desire the office of Bishop, he desireth a good work." The Minister was talking to him, at the far corner of the veranda, talking and talking while something like white foam was forming at both corners of his mouth. But he went on talking and talking and ignored the accretions.

And the man came rolling into the driveway, late one evening, traveling like a cat, as they say, over the loose gravel of white road, to the house he paid for. Her house stood on the kiss of a steep hill which looked arrogantly into the sea, and on the way down there were many bushes, some of which had names, but he never was good at names and bushes. And farther down the hill the sheep were rolling and they had wool on their backs but the wool was thick with their shit and urine and nobody thought of ever shearing the sheep, the sheep were for meat and for making rotis; but he never liked sheep and he came rolling like the plains beneath the hill into her house, to find her naked in the living room, lying on the floor that had three scatter rugs, and music from French Canada on the record player. The man was a big man; they used to say that he was a brilliant man with tinges of madness, a man who used to be able to look you in your eyes with his bloodshot large eyes, looking at you that way to make you know how important and powerful he really was. He was a powerful man, his build told you so. And he came into the woman's

*house for which he paid the price, and knelt down on his hands
and knees, and milked the living juices of her body, strong in
his mouth, from the large sophisticated udder between her legs.
And when the milking was over, she turned over, and then she
turned the record over, and out came medieval music, with her
turn at the milking of the classical chords. The sea could be
heard from that steep distance, with the sheep grazing on the
brown hill where there were only stones and pebbles and his
own two stones. And it was in this frame both of the window
and of mind, that a man with a camera came up to the louvers
of the expensive unsafe house, lowered them a little, and blew
one bubble of electronic light through the frame of the louvers
and caught him, and the woman, forever in that posture, for
posterity. One of these photographs was shown by Weekesie.
She was like a bitch dead and stiff standing erect on her four
legs . . .*

He stirred in his sleep which had come on so suddenly, and was so restful. He turned over on his right
side, put his hand out to touch the alarm clock which
would soon be going off, for the office. But he touched
hair all over his pillow. And he felt the body tangled
between his legs, and he knew where he was; that he was
safe and that he had not come as she had asked him. It
was now a time of disappointment that he was not in his
own bed. She drew her legs tightly around his body, and
he could feel her fingers like feathers, and he could smell
her breath on his face, as if she was about to feed him
something she held in her mouth; and they stayed like
that just for a moment, and then she rode him like a cock-
horse towards another victory conquering Banbury Cross
in the earlier two rhythms of their bodies into one rocking
chair. He could feel her coming near, like the climb up
the hill with the sheep, and he could feel the exertion and
her anger at his slow progress; but the rate of progress
was relative to exhaustion and her fatigue rung out like a
dishrag of this hard sweet labor; and then *she* came, in an

arrival of consummate noise and victory; and she screamed over the playing of the music from the dining room, ignoring the neighbors, "Oh Jesus *Christ!*"

He had never ever experienced such shame in love . . . *A long line of policemen dressed in their formal wear of blue-black serge, wearing their black peaked caps with the broad line of red around them, marched out of the station, with their guns in their hands, ready and loaded to face the crowd of people from the city, listening to the grass-roots politicians; the people were angry and were shouting about the high cost of chickens and salt fish and corned beef in the country. In their midst was the grass-roots politician, Kwame, exhorting them to begin with the large store at the bottom of Market Square, just a spit's throw from where they lived behind this main thoroughfare, and end with the smallest store which sold gold, frankincense and myrrth, at the other end of the city. And Kwame told them to make sure that when they were finished, when it was all over, that they had enough cash in their hands and in their homes, locked in the hiding places under the bed, because when the "big boys" came to work early on Monday morning, in two days, all credit would be cut off, just like they would be cutting off heads and balls and hands and life. By the time the long black line of policemen reached the Market Square, the crowd had grown twice in size and violence, and the policemen were faced with either shooting them with the pistles of bulls and Hitler, or watching them; and the policemen decided to hold their guns in their hands like giant penises, for a while savoring both feel and comfort, and then they put down their guns and joined the crowd, because chickens and corned beef and salt fish were the same price for them, and they were flying through windows with the people, with corned beef and biscuits in their hands, in their pockets, in their mouths, in their helmets, in their underwear and in their panties.*

The woman was lying beside him, fagged-out and tired from her unrequited single lonely journey; and she rolled sympathetically closer to quiet the disturbance in his unorganized, unorgasmed body.

"Shoot! Shoot! Shoot!"

It was in his sleep that he was crying out for the power and prowess which he did not have. And it scared her a little; it might have scared her less if she had been awakened by this command, when it poured into her body. But she ran her hands over his face and then his body and kissed his lips and then climbed on top of him, and began to move her body in a slow grinding rhythm, with her eyes closed so he wouldn't have to see his disappointment in her face, and she was saying, over and over, "Don't let them take that away from you, don't let them take that away from you ... "

It was "that" too, he was beginning to understand, that the country was taking away from him. Power in the country remained power. Plain, raw and visceral and vicious. There was nothing he could see that made any difference between the means and the ends. Everything was ends. *The Lord giveth and the Lord taketh away.* The paradise had reverted back to the plantation. No one ever questioned the historical meaning and the contemporary appropriateness of the quotation, as if they knew it applied to the power over them: the power to give and the power to take. Kwame knew that it applied to death. Kwame said that the man who first applied its common scriptural usage to politics had deliberately extracted from it all the meaning it might have had previously, and in turn applied to it, in terms of power, a natural dispensation of favor. It was the ends. It was the power to be "terminated" from a chairmanship; to be "terminated" by a chairman; the power to be disgraced, like Juliet; the power to step and stomp on a flower; the power to be branded a "fool," or a "bandit;" the power to be a fool: "Any fool who spends sixteen years studying law must, through the Law of Torts, average into a fool, and eventually become a foolish lawyer!"

The woman was breathing harder now: she was like one of the sheep who has to get to the top of the hill in a certain sweet short time, with compulsion and forcefulness and because of physiology; and because of the land, she has lain too often on the man who is now beneath her. So her eyes must be wild and she must hold her lips tight like the approbation of a desire; and her lips must become a slice of malice and frustration, in its own moratorium. Some day she must, however, open her eyes, or have them opened for her by the alternation of energy and breath, for she has stopped breathing too long, in that one moment it takes before her exhaustion erupts in its explosion of sperms and new generation. And when she does exhale and explode, like the moment of death, it will be more violent than an orgasm, and will explode in *"Fuck you!"*

HOW should this poem begin? How could he begin it? *Of Man's first disobedience, and fruit Of that forbidden tree, whose mortal taste Brought death into the world, and all our woe, With loss of Eden . . .* Was that Eden in the same dispensation as this "paradise?" And had he sinned with the woman? He could not have, since there was no orgasm to consummate the loss of his Eden . . . He had already used five sheets of paper, and could decide on only one word for the poem: "Barbarian." Barbarian was so close to other words which sounded like it.

> *I, who ere while the happy garden sung*
> *By one Man's disobedience lost, now sing*
> *Recover'd Paradise to all mankind,*
> *By one Man's firm obedience fully tried*
> *Through all temptation, and the Tempter foil'd*
> *In all his wiles,* defeated and repuls'd,
> *And Eden rais'd in the waste wilderness . . .*

It had been said already, and by greater poets: the regaining of paradise. So he gave up thinking about the poem. For writing a poem was not the same thing as defining words; and he was now spending too much time with words.

The telephone rang, and he was glad for the interruption. He was becoming increasingly uneasy with the sudden falling of light and dusk in the country, and the street on which he lived was, in more ways than its physical layout, a dead-end street. He was glad for the interruption.

"Listen, don't say nothing. Let me do all the talking. You know who it is?" It was Kwame. *"They* have tapped your line. The lines o' certain people have been tap." He wanted to know why; but Kwame, who knew the nuances of language better, had advised him not to talk. "Lemme do the talking. You remember that meeting that we had down at the beach house? Well, that is pure danger, my Brother. Pure danger. I've been talking to certain people who tell me that the Minister have something up his sleeve. What he has up his sleeve is that he wants to be prime minister. Now, in order for him to be prime minister, he got to get your boss, the minister in culture, outta the way. He needs the rich boys, the merchant boys, on his side. You hear about that report, the report dealing with making the country into a more better place for poor people to get jobs after they finish school? You read that report, yet?"

"Which report exactly are you . . . "

"Man, I tell you don't talk! That report approved. The cabinet meet today, and they approve it. Ten ministers vote for, and this one minister vote against, 'cause the way he figuring, is that if he back the report, then he lose the support of the big boys who backing him. And this is where you come in. You come in in this way. You're suppose to be the man who is going to make things look bad for the country. They are planning to make you responsible for what happen, and what don't happen. You is the scrapegoat. *The scrapegoat.* I went to that meeting at the beach house, thinking it was going to give the people cheaper salt fish. But that meeting isn't anything to do with what they planning now. Chalk and cheese, my Brother. Now, lissen good to this. This is where you come in again. Rumors are going 'bout the place to the effect that you come back here to start a black power revolution. The Minister himself spreading that rumor. He say you are turning the culture of this country into a black power culture. And lemme tell you something else. That stick-licking thing that the minister o' culture want you to write the report on, well that is pure shite. Man, stick-licking went out with slavery, and the only people, the *onliest* people in this day and age who indulge in that blasted foolishness, is the tourist board people, with their donkey-cart rides and shite like that, all over the city. The Third World is laughing at us, my Brother. We is the comedians to the Third World, and to people like Angola, Africa and Mozambique. We is the comedians of the Third World." He was out of breath. He talked the same way now as he talked on the platform. John Moore had to listen carefully. "Are you still there, my Brother?"

"Yeah, yeah . . . "

"Okay! I going ask you a very serious question now. Are you in possession of a gun?"

"A gun?"

"Something yuh does shoot people with! A gun."

"Are you telling me that I need . . . "

"Get a fucking gun, my Brother! Get a *wompuh*, a gun, in case they come after you . . . "

For a while longer, John Moore held the telephone in his hand, expecting the voice to continue talking.

The humidity in the room was stifling. He unbuttoned the first two buttons on his shirt-jack top, but he did not feel any livelier. He was not scared. He was merely displaced. Alone. Standing within that space which determined madness from sanity. He could have been anywhere, for he was not capable of comprehending. Or he could be, simply, here, right here, on this hill, in this house, in this beautiful land with the valley which opens itself to the approaching planes, with its lawns on which the women stand like African and Eastern queens and princesses, and sip their drinks and hold their glasses with the correct number of fingers, and do not worry about the men or about their sexual appetites, because they know that they rule this beautiful land, because of those very sexual appetites: *Of that forbidden tree whose mortal taste brought death into the world* . . .

Power? Or the corruption of power? All the power he had came from the reputation of the poet. And they were, in this country, really only words. Words. Kwame's telephone message had contradicted the philosophy that the pen is greater than the sword. In this country it was the sword, for *the Lord giveth and the Lord taketh!* and that itself connoted death, and the sword.

He had left all the louvers open. He hastened to close them now. He switched off all the lights on the outside of the house.

He made a drink of scotch and water, very strong. And then he sat in his favorite chair.

Sitting there, he tried to make sense out of the warning. It was too unusual. All the sense he could make out of it was that the people in this country had a different sense of use for the telephone: it was like an extension of their tongues.

The telephone rang again. This time it did not startle him.

"Hello?"

"Your-humble-servant, here! Can't rest God-almighty's eyes on yuh these days, son. Have you finished the paper? Well, never mind, 'cause I don't need it anymore. How's tricks?"

"Fine, fine."

"I was in cabinet all day. Hard labor, son. Don't let nobody fool you and ask you to be a minister. You keep-on writing them po-ems, son. Oh, by the way. Although I don't need the paper, I still need your research notes. I could use them. Taxpayers' money, son, taxpayers' money. I going catch-up with you, boy."

He realized that he had hardly touched the drink. The humidity had already caused a ring of water to be formed around the bottom of the glass. He had no desire for the drink. He didn't know what to do now. But he knew that he needed someone to talk to. At eleven-thirty at night, not many people would be awake. And he could not just call anyone, and discuss his fears on the telephone. Now, if the woman . . .

The long-distance operator came on the line while he heard the hum of miles over the Atlantic. He was calling the tenant in his house in Toronto.

– Hey, Brother! I thought you would never call! How's the motherfucking Prime Minister, and how's tricks going-down down there in the land of paradise? Hey, man . . . guess who I saw?

– Go into my study, and you will see a book called *White Dog*. Look on the shelf on the southern wall, I think it's the second shelf from the top. I'll hold . . .

– Now, what do I do with this book, now? Send it to you on the wire?

– Open it. Open it on page seven or eight . . . begin at the paragraph . . .

– I got it . . . "There *is something deeply demoralizing and disturbing in those sudden transformations of a familiar being, man or animal, into a total stranger. It is one of those moments when your reassuring little world flies to pieces . . .* "

– Turn to the section where they talk about the dog and the black people.

– Let me see . . . you know this is the first time something like this has ever been asked of me! . . . Here it is . . . "*This dog had been trained especially to attack blacks. No, I'm not imagining things. Every time a Negro comes near the door, he goes mad. Vicious. With whites, nothing happens. He wags his tail and shakes his head . . .*

– Thank you.

– What the hell's going on down there, Brother?

– I am talking, sir, from observances, sir. I'm talking from observances . . .

– Are you freaking-out on me, Brother?

The drink of scotch and water he had fixed some

time ago was still there. Moths had lighted on the rim of
the glass, and some had already been drowned inside it.
He studied their fate, and his comprehension of it. His
interpretation of their fate went no further. They were
just dead moths. No longer silken as in their interrupted
youth; no longer pests; and the woman's clothes would
be safe. In what ways could the quotation be applied to
them? A lake was gathering around the bottom of the
glass; and as he studied this, merely its present dramatic
situation, he saw an ant crawl across the table top, at first
cautiously, then in a wild scramble, and it collided with
the water and itself was drowned. The sudden and significant destruction of these unimportant bodies — he
could hardly call them beings — worried him; and he
wondered what broader application he would give to
them. What lessons in care and self-preservation, after
the two telephone conversations tonight, was this
drowned ant pointing out to him? *Go to the ant, thou
sluggard.* Was this the scope of his comprehension of
things around him? Of persons and situations which all
seem to crush in on him without purpose? Without
rhyme? They crowded his reality with the kind of
rhythm of which he was not ofay. But what rhythm suitable to the cold land from which he had come could he
use to go along with the tempo of this place? *Consider
her ways and be wise.* The ant. There was never any good
poem written about the moth. The moth was almost lifeless while it lived. It certainly was bloodless. Nobody
had bothered to attribute an emotion, only mothballs, in
the writing of a poem to a moth. But the ant — the poem
called the ant a "she," a woman. In this country, where
women outnumbered men almost two to one, the ant
would be referred to as a "he." But the poet had called
the ant a she.

The telephone had been ringing while he was
deep in the construction of the ant. When he picked it

up, expecting anything now, the voice hit his ears immediately, not permitting him the courtesy of saying hello.

"I'm worried about you," she said. "I've been
calling you all night. There's something I have to talk
with you that can't wait till morning. Can I come to you?
... or are you too tired to come down the hill?"

It was all over the city. When he passed in his car, people stood to look at him, and pointed in his direction. But he traveled too fast to read their faces; he was not sure whether their expressions said pity, or disgust. When he came to work one morning, and for the next few mornings after that first day, his staff held their heads down as he passed. When they had to see him in his office, they cut their appointments short. It was all over the city, and the country. People were saying, "The new director o' culture is a radical, man!" And some said, "He bringing vi'lence and guns in the country!"

An article published originally many years before in a Toronto magazine was reprinted and rewritten in the *Weekly*. The original article was an interview that John Moore had done with Malcolm X, when the latter was national leader of the Black Muslims in America. The *Weekly* used John Moore's questions, but without the question marks after them. His questions were thereby turned into inflammatory remarks. The article was headed "ANGRIEST BLACK POWER MAN NOW BASED AT HOME" and was written by the editor. John Moore disregarded this crude manipulation, which was quite ordinary for the *Weekly*. And he therefore miscalculated that the readers of the paper would be able to see that it was an attempt at character assassination. He also miscalculated the power of the printed word, in a country where the printed newspaper word was glorified as truth. The entire nation believed the article. The politicians in the Other party deliberately said nothing about the article; and those in the government confused the situation further by saying, "At this time, we have no comment to make on Mr. John Moore's ideology." He was virtually killed by their "no comment."

He waited that first morning in his office for a call from the ministry. But no call came. Nobody came to him and said, "Now, what the hell are you doing, Johnmoore?" Not even that. No one questioned the truth, or the lies, in the article. The woman called him and said, "From now on, you better understand that *they* won't be calling you no more! Or seeing you!" That is the way it is done, she told him. "You are alone, from now on, from now-on."

It was as if a contract had been placed on his life. He would remain there, wilting in the humidity of fear, or of anxiety, until the blow was delivered. He thought of his friend Weekesie. What had they really done to Weekesie? Did they really poison him, as the woman insisted they had done? He would never know the truth; for, as she also insisted, there was not going to be an autopsy. All he would ever know about Weekesie, and about Byron Pond, was the accumulation of all the rumors. The officials and the politicians never discussed these matters outside of their cliques. He belonged to none of these cliques. So he would be left, also, to wilt in the fear of ignorance.

Passing along the corridor at the Department of National Culture, he overheard Vagabond saying, "Man, I did always expect that that damn man, Johnmoore, would turn in a blasted disruption!" Vagabond saw him, knew that he had overheard the remark, then smiled and bowed very low and respectfully, and said, "Morning, Chief!" This kind of deceit, John Moore thought, was fascinating; the ends, that's what it was, the *ends*. The ends were played out the same way, from the bottom of the scale right up to the top. "I going have to tell the Prime Minister about this," Vagabond said, as John Moore walked past. It was as if the country had been joined in a common consciousness to be vicious.

"Be-Jesus Christ, I could have tell all o' you-all, all o' this would have happen when you make a colored man the director! Yuh can't put a black man in charge o' nothing nowadays in these days o' inflation, man! Put a black man in charge, and every-blasted-thing is deflated. Look at Amin. Look at Nkrumah. Look at Lumumba. Look at we own minister o' trade . . . be-Jesus Christ, yuh can't even buy corned beef and salt fish nowadays, since they change him from a kiss-me-arse barefoot boy walking 'bout here, into a minister o' government. You see it now for yourselves. You see it? Them is facts, and observances! He that hath eyes to see, rass-hole see. Whenever you put a colored man in a big important position, and give him some power, he must turn-into a rass-hole radical. The philosophies o' socialism prove that, man. It isn' *me* talking. Well, look at Stalin and Trotsky, then! And if yuh want more proof, look-back at Kwame Nkrumah! Look at the entire world o' colonialism and neocolonialism. A black power revolution in this democratic country? Not for shite! Not when it is the white people they going start killing-off, the same white people who is responsible for putting food in our mouths, and in our children's mouths. The same white people who have been so good over the years o' history and slavery to the colored people in this country, one of which, mind you, one of which, is the same bastard, Johnmoore! All this disruption is running-up the national debt and running out the tourisses. But all I got to say is this: let Johnmoore lift a gun and start something in this country. Let me *hear* that Johnmoore talk any more shite 'bout revolution, and you will see if I, *me*, won't be the first man to pelt a big rock in his fucking face! He calling himself a *angry radical?* He is a radical? Man, this place was a staple, peaceable, the most freest country in the whole whirrrrl, before he come back here. It is a better place for having three percentage white people living here, with ninety-seven percentage power, controlling the fucking Prime Minister o' this country. And that situation is better than any grass-roots government. What we want a grass-roots for? You don't see it my way? Man, tell me, man, wha' you think?"

And on the day after, a letter appeared in the Letters to the Editor column, dealing with the same subject.

"This country has prided itself on three hundred and more years of uninterrupted English institutions and culture. In that time, we have seen our dear land flourish, and today we are a democracy within the sound framework of the British Commonwealth of Nations. Radicalism of whatever form has been kept at bay in this country for too long for some foreign interloper to come with these strange philosophies of radicalism now. Signed, Civitus."

At this point John Moore was still consoling himself; he would tell the public, if he got the chance, that they were seeing the matter the wrong way. But the country had the highest literacy rate in the world. The freest country and the most literate country. He rationalized their reaction as temporary madness; or was it blindness, a kind of Daltonism?

He decided to act.

Just to think about it frightened him. It was the first positive act he would take upon himself to perpetrate.

He drove to the Government Broadcasting Service and emptied all the bile, all the frustrations, all the knots that had been tied up in his system since he arrived in the country. Within fifteen minutes of the start of the interview, reporters from the newspapers entered the studio and began taking notes.

"I am a poet," he declared. "I am a poet." And he answered all their questions about radicalism, about black power, about "The Rate of Exchange;" and he told them over and over, "I am a poet."

The general manager of GBS thanked him for coming forward: "If we only had ten more men like you . . . " and told him to make sure that he watched at nine o'clock that night for the television showing of his interview.

"*I am a poet.*"

It had been done. He didn't know it was so easy to act.

That night at nine o'clock he was alone in front of the television. The television came on, and he saw the Minister, "Your-humble-servant," full-face on the screen. The Minister smiled, and began to speak. "Now, ladies and gentlemen, I don't come before you tonight to talk about revolution." He paused, and smiled churlishly. "Revolution, as you know, is something that we've never had in this country. And something we don't want. Well, look. Lemme put it this way to you. Lemme put it so that all o' you would understand what I mean, by saying that I really can't understand all this revolution-talk making the rounds in this country." He paused again, and smiled. "How many of you-all out there in television-land, as they say up North . . . " He paused and smiled his broad smile. One eye was almost completely closed as he smiled. "How many of you ever see a gun? A simple thing like a gun? How many o' you ever *fired* a gun?" He disappeared momentarily from view. John Moore imagined that the camera was malfunctioning. But immediately after, the Minister reappeared, in a larger close-up, larger than the screen. He was holding a .38 revolver to his head.

He smiled again. He squeezed the trigger. And the gun made a sharp noise. And he said, "Is this what wunnuh want to see in your city? In your neighborhood? In your village? In your country?"

The startled journalists at the press table burst out laughing. The cameras panned from them to the largest close-up of the Minister.

The Minister was not smiling now. And he had not answered his own question. He did not have to; and words, anyway, were not necessary now.

Tears were running down his face. The close-up was held for a long time, and then the technician, realizing what was happening, faded the image from the screen. And in its place, "Trouble is Temporary" filled the screen . . .

She was silent throughout the drive from his house to the main police station, where he was going to take out a license for a gun. She parked the car in a space which had "Superintendent of Detectives" marked on the black macadam.

"Have you ever used one o' these things before?" an officer asked him.

He wanted to appear innocent of violence. "No," he said, "I haven't even held a gun in my hand before. When I was in the Cadet Corps, well, as you know, we used to use board rifles . . . "

"I hope you don't shoot your blasted self, then!" And the officer laughed and the woman laughed.

They had chosen the gun from a haberdashery establishment. "Shoot any bastard who you suspect. Don't think twice about it. All you got to do is drag the bastard from the house, off your property, and leave him laying by the road."

He now had a gun. And a box of shells for it. He started to imagine prowlers and people coming to take his life. He wondered whether he would have the nerve to shoot a man, dead. Kill him. He was walking the street filled with black people, his own countrymen, and he was carrying a loaded .38 revolver pushed in his trousers waist, touching his flesh; and he was feeling scared that any time it would go off.

"Does this thing have a safety catch?"

"Didn't the police show you?"

A woman selling oranges looked up from her tray, recognized him, and shouted, "You black bitch! You come to this peaceable place to start a revolution?" She called out to her neighbor, "Look-he! Look-he! The revolution-fellow! You didn't watch television last night?"

She squeezed his hand comfortingly. He wondered whether she too would turn against him; whether she would *have* to turn against him? How long would it take her? But he felt the stronger pressure of her grip on his hand, and he knew she was appealing to his confidence.

"You have your gun, now. I hope you know how to use it." She waited long enough for him to see the point; and when she thought that he had, that he had remembered the night they had spent together in the four-poster, she smiled with him.

The gun was rubbing against his thigh. What a strange thing to happen! A gun rubbing against his thigh. In *Esquire*, it must have been in 1970, there was an article written by Jean Genet about the fat thighs of policemen and the size of their guns. Genet was really talking about other things, not only the sizes of guns and thighs. But this gun rubbing against his thigh . . .

"This is your country," she said, sipping her sherry. They had stopped at a tourist bar for a drink. "I want you to remember that. This is your country."

He sat and watched her, this woman, with all her courage and with such basic common sense; and still so exposed by caring for him, and loving him. "Are you satisfied that that woman, that whore on the hill where we went that night, could come from wherever the hell she comes from . . . South Africa, is it? . . . and do her work here? And *you* can't? You tell me you can't? The papers are even calling her a national artist, these days. How do you explain that?"

He sat and watched her.

"You can't answer that one; can you?"

"You hate her, don't you?"

"I don't have to hate her. This is *my* country, so we aren't equals, so I don't have to hate *her!*"

"You're becoming a racist."

"Do you think I could go to South Africa and behave the way she behaves in my country?" She sipped her sherry, since there was no way of putting the point better. She was toasting her own logic. "Her son, who wasn't even born here, gets the best education this country can offer. *Free*. Taxpayers' money. And not one blind cent of that educational investment on those two racists will ever come back to this poor country. Do you think those things are right?"

"But the education is free to everybody, isn't it?"

She put down her glass, and looked straight at him. "To me, she is *nobody!*"

She sipped her sherry, and the taste seemed to transform her mood, and the feeling and the movement in her face changed. "Christ, man, I really *love you* . . . " She looked very beautiful then. "I forgot to tell you I heard that the Americans are giving money to that man who was criticizing the government at the political meeting — Kwame, I mean." How long had she had this information? He was watching her closely. If he watched more closely, he would see when a change of mood overtook her; and he would learn to see the reflection of things in her face. "Oh look! Look over there!" When he turned, he saw only the back of a man walking away. "That's *him!*"

John Moore looked at the man. He was wearing a badly fitting shirt-jack top, and dark trousers. He was moving heavily, and swaying like a ship laden with a shifting ballast. His sleeves were short, and John Moore could see the fashionable wristwatch like a chunk of gold. There was perspiration on the man's face. He was about five feet ten or eleven inches; perhaps six feet. And you would readily agree that he was tall if it were not for the shape of his body. He walked like a man who was drunk. Beside him was a slightly built woman, whose manner of gesticulating when she talked placed her by birth somewhere in Europe; Switzerland, or France, or even Germany. Her hair was long and reddish brown. The man held her arm, and had turned her round to face them, to search for a place. Her face was really pimply. And not particularly beautiful or attractive. The man held her in a sort of embrace. But the embrace might not have been one of love. He could have been shielding her from the eyes of the waiters. He was a man, the woman said, who hid things from people; although he boasted that he could go into the most crowded market in the city and push his hand into the bottom of a brine barrel and pull out the best pieces of salt-cured pig tails, which he also boasted he cooked better than any woman in the whole country. He was a damn good cook, she said. They were within two tables of John Moore and the woman; and there they sat down. He was wearing his dark glasses and they made him look something like a bandit in the movies. But when he wiped the perspiration from his face, and took off his dark glasses, he still looked like a bandit; without the perspiration. He had walked in life like a man who had no principles, she said. But you knew also that he was a man of some position in the country. And because you knew that, you knew he could be seen drunk in public. He walked, you would conclude with that knowledge of position and size and importance, like a seal. Or as if his bunions gave him trouble. He had to move from side to side before he could move an inch forward.

"That's the Prime Minister!" she said, when it was safe to whisper. "Now you see what kind o' man he is!"

John Moore saw that he had never met the man face to face; he had always seen him when he was leaving, from behind, as if this was going to be the disposition of their relationship. He was troubled that he had never seen the leader of his country from the front, face to face . . .

It was time to go. He seemed to be always leaving one place to go to another: there was never any time to sit down and relax. "Julie called me," she said, apologizing to him that Julie had called. "Julie called me two days ago, and said that he wants to speak with you. He said there's something you ought to know, but he didn't tell me what it is. He's coming to see you he said . . . "

A car was following them as they pulled out of the parking lot of the tourist bar. Dusk had fallen. It was what the native people call "a dark night," a night without a moon. But going through the city streets, he could see the uncollected garbage which spilled out of the concrete stuff-bins; boxes and dead cats and lots of soiled pieces of paper; and of course the dogs. There were always dogs: dogs in the streets, dogs lying in the middle of the road late at night, as if they wanted to die, as if they were dead; dead dogs stiff and bloated, healthier looking now that they were dead than when they lived, scrawny and picking a meal from the stuff-bins. "I don't really understand," she said, "why there is always so much garbage where the poor people live. You have to pass through all this blasted garbage to get anywhere in this place!"

The car was still following them at a safe distance. "Julie was telling me," she said, "that you should be careful with Kwame. He talks too much."

They were in front of her house now, and she turned the engine off, and remained sitting. He felt she had something on her mind. But he did not know how to get it out of her, so he sat back in the seat and closed his eyes. He felt her stir, and he opened his eyes to see that a car had drawn up beside them. It was dark. Only the outlines of things could be distinguished in this night without a moon.

The man driving the car rolled down his window, and said, "Pssssst! Brother-man, it's me, man!" He knew who it was. Kwame.

"Talk about the devil," she said.

"Man, I followed you, man, to talk to you. Goodnight, Mistress," he greeted the woman, who sucked on her teeth, showing her annoyance. "Is only me, Mistress. I have something to tell Johnmoore. I followed your car all up here, 'cause I didn' want to miss Johnmoore. Hope you weren't frighten' having me following you so, Mistress. One o' those things, yuh know."

"I'll wait in the car," she said. And before he got out, she made a signal to him to inquire whether he was wearing his gun. He had forgotten that he was now a different man. He became aware of the heavy coldish gun rubbing against his thigh.

"Come in my car, man," Kwame said. "Yuh can't be too careful these days, and if a car pass and see me talking to you, you can never tell which kind o' rumor would start-up 'bout that . . . "

John Moore kept his hand on the gun. He thought he should probably have taken it out and held it in his hand, under his shirt-jack top. But perhaps it was safe just to have his hand touching it, just in case . . .

"I heard you got the gun," Kwame said. John Moore became more uneasy. "I hope you walking with your gun, 'cause all hell just break-loose, my Brother. There's a fellow on your staff, Vagabond? He spreading rumors. He went in your office tonight. That's why I followed you. They stole all your files, and I hear they took them to the Prime Minister, and . . . "

"What?"

"Believe me, Brother-man. Trust the grass-roots man. They want me to hold a meeting and attack you as a radical. But I tell them, go to hell, me and your father grow-up together in this place. But all them files in your office now in the hands o' the Prime Minister."

"That's alright. There's nothing confidential in them anyway."

"But that isn' the point, my Brother! That is not the point. Files is files. A man who don't like you could do *anything* in this whirl to a file. Files is changed every day in this country, Moorey, man. Even a little man like me does get a peep at government files once in a while, on a Thursday night, in a certain rum shop in the city. Man, how you think I gets my information on this government? We even changed a few things in one o' them, man!"

"Thank you. I'd better get to my office."

"No, don't do that. They may be setting a trap for you. Don't do that. Lissen to the grass-roots man. I just left there, before I was following you. And I recognize a security police fellow up there, waiting in the dark in a car. That security fellow is a right-hand man belonging to the Minister, the same Minister who invited you to the meeting at the beach house, and who asked me to hold a meeting to lambast you as a radical. So, don't do that. Don't go back to the office tonight."

He could feel the gun rubbing against his thigh.

"You go straight home and keep your gun cocked. I don't want to frighten yuh, but between me and you, Johnmoore, I think that man the Minister, you know who I mean . . . Your-humble-servant, that one . . . I think he gunning for you, I think he out to get you, or something . . . "

"When are they having the meeting?"

"If I was you, I wouldn't go. I will bring you the information. I really can't understand what going on, though, 'cause I joined the hoonta-thing, as they calls it, because I want the poor people to get cheaper salt fish and jobs, but I don't understand how this thing turning-out, at all, man . . . "

"Keep me informed, then."

"Man, how you mean! As man, man! I getting back in touch tonight." He himself opened the door to let John Moore out; and this was puzzling. It should have been the other way round. "Oh, by the way,

Brother-man, you going be here . . . at the Mistress . . . or you going be home?"

John Moore could see the trap, could see many traps, could see many faces: but were they traps? "I'll be here."

"Mistress, goodnight," Kwame said, and drove off.

She remained sitting in her car, with her head on her folded hands over the steering wheel. She sighed, and he felt it was an expression of her own danger, that she was beginning to realize and to feel the danger in their association.

"It's getting to you, isn't it?" he asked her.

"Take me to your home." This time he did not tell her that he had some poems to revise.

He entered his house from a long winding driveway. Over this driveway, for the first few yards, hung branches of the red and pink bougainvillea. It could be dark and dangerous at the beginning of the driveway, especially when there was no moon. There was no moon tonight. And at the end of the driveway, at the carport, it was dark. And it could be dangerous. For immediately beyond the carport, at the side where the lawn dipped down, that whole portion of grass was covered by the overhanging bushes; and a man could wait there for him, and throw a stone in his face, or shoot him. The pipe and the hose for watering the large lawn were there in the back. There was a light switch in the carport, but he never left this light burning, for it exposed him as an easy target. He would turn on this light only when he arrived home with company; or with the woman, as he was tonight. The other side of the house, on his left hand as he entered, was dark too. And there were crawling vines and more flowers on the roof of the patio. He liked to have breakfast on this patio. The mornings were bright, and the air was fresh, and this seemed to do something both to his appetite and to his taste. But the house was unsafe. The louvers could be opened from the outside. And if they proved noisy for the intruder, the entire frame could be taken out with a screwdriver. He had tested this one afternoon. He had taken out one frame and reassembled it within four minutes. The maid had been scrubbing the hallway; and by the time she had come back into the kitchen to change the water, he had completed it; and she had not heard him.

The woman drove the car right into the carport. During the drive from her house she had not spoken once. The GBS was off a long time ago, so there was not even that distraction to make the journey, and her company, more bearable.

He got out, and stood to wait for her, when with no warning she reversed the car, turned out of the driveway, and disappeared out of sight. He stood there, trying to understand why she would do a thing like that. Her headlights disappeared, and the night became peace; and only the noises of that time of night — an occasional dog barking on the hill where the low-income houses were, or an early fowl-cock — told him that he was not standing in this driveway alone in the world, that the entire neighborhood was not dead. Then he heard her footsteps over the loose gravel just before the solid cement of the entrance to the driveway; and he relaxed in the darkness. She came up to him, and said, in the serious manner she had developed to utter caution and fear and love, "Cars are too obvious a sign to let somebody know you're home. I parked it down the road." His own car was in the garage for the weekend. "That man may come back," she added, "and you don't want to be taken by surprise." Cars had become, she said, not only status symbols in the country; they could tell you whether a certain person was visiting the wrong house, and that knowledge was usually the basis for gossip. She was protecting him from gossip as well as from danger.

The woman went inside the house. "Been a long day! I hope Kwame comes soon ... "

He remained for a long time thinking beside the kitchen door entrance. The fragrance from the flowers made him aware that he was still outside. It was warm but still comfortable.

He walked back to the lawn where it was darkest. The hose was rambling over the lawn like a green harmless snake. And the pipe was shut tight. He stood there and looked into the darkness, down the ravine, right over the rise in the thick guinea-grass pasture, out to the sea which he could not really see, but knew was there, only because it was there last night. He moved around to the other side of the house, under the covered roof of dried coconut fronds and climbing chalices. And he sat down on one of the patio chairs made out of iron like the bars at the windows and the doors of the other houses in the area.

A lizard was climbing among the half-dead leaves of the chalice vine, and the crackling noise stirred him. He had forgotten the woman inside the house. He tried to see the lizard. And wondered whether lizards slept at night, whether they knew how to sleep. When he was a boy . . . when he was a boy in this country . . . *Briggs and Mickey and I climbed the clammy-cherry tree in the girls' school yard, and came down with three fat green lizards which all had large yellow-and-green combs under their chins. "Kill-he! Kill-he quick!" Briggs said. He always wanted to be a surgeon. "Hold-he-down, then!" Mickey said, who said he was going to become a druggist. And I, of no known ambition, held them down, and we cut them up and open, cutting out heart first, and then other "insides." And we packed them, with cloth from our mothers' rags, in the long cigarette boxes which we used as coffins. We had first made three oval holes in them, for the mourners, "the little boys," to see the faces of the dead. And we put pieces of camphor into the "coffin-boxes." The camphor was stolen from somebody's mother who worked at the hotel nearby. And then we got our "cars," made out of an axle to which two wheels made from shoe-polish tins were nailed and oiled and greased, and a longer piece of stick, perhaps also from the clammy-cherry tree, nailed on to the axle; and we buried the "deads." "Only our memories of this country are beautiful, and free, apart from the land, the natural land," she used to say when they were driving through the country districts and stopped for a drink, on a hill, to see one entire half of the country at their feet. "Man, put-down the*

man's lizard! That is the man's lizard. He kill-he himself, and
prepare it for burying, and thing. Put-down the man's dead,
that is the man's funeral, man . . . "

"Mr. Moore? Mr. Moore?"

His maid was standing over him. At first he
thought she was a nurse; he thought he was in a hospital.
She was dressed in her white uniform.

It was already morning.

"Mr. Moore, I could hear you from way-out there
in the road, as I was coming in."

She had apparently not entered the house yet. He
searched for his keys in his pocket. The gun touched his
fingers. And the woman, in the house . . .

"But you mean to tell me, Mr. Moore, that you
spend the whole entire night out here, by yourself?
Nowadays, Mr. Moore? It's not safe out here, Mr. Moore.
I don't know what's happening to this man at all . . . "

He could hear her muttering to herself as she
unlocked the patio gate to enter the house; and then she
opened windows and doors to give the house "an air-
ing," as she always said. " . . . They not giving this poor
gentleman a chance at all, at all. I don't understand why
they picking on this man . . . I can't see nothing wrong
with this man . . . " Along with her mumbling was the
noise of plates and pans as she prepared breakfast.

And the woman came out on to the patio, and
stretched, and rubbed her eyes. "I couldn't wait anymore. I couldn't stay awake with you. Anybody came
last night?"

He rubbed his eyes. In the chalice vines were
many lizards. They sat looking at him out of one eye;
and when that eye must have become blurred, they
turned around over the crackling dying branches, and
stared at him some more. Long yellow-and-green things
came down under their necks, and their eyes winked
open and shut, with water in them.

He did not know where he was. He could have
been in a plane, he could have been in Toronto; and even
though he had seen the maid, and this woman was now
standing before him in the clothes in which she had
slept, it was as if he had thought he had seen someone
who resembled maid and woman at the same time; and
he was not sure. All he knew was that he was seeing
lizards with yellow things under their necks. He felt
very frightened, even though he was not alone now, and
isolated and without any feeling that he had sat all night
in the exposed chair, or as if he was somewhere else; he
felt as if there were no roots growing underneath him . . .

That so very beautiful black woman with the soft silken skin blessed in his memory of her, with the name Nefertiti, was splashing about in the shallow water. He saw her legs for the first time, naked and strong up to her thighs. Her thighs were the future of other black generations of her country . . .

The first person who wanted to see him that morning in his office was Vagabond. He wanted to know if he could get an advance on his salary.

"As you know, sir, I am the lowest man on the totem-pole."

John Moore was thinking of what Kwame had said; and here was the best chance he could have of testing the accuracy of Kwame's information. But Vagabond's crude manner made him uncomfortable; and if it was true that Vagabond had such close connections with the Prime Minister, then he would have to be tactful in dealing with him. But was he really afraid of Vagabond, or was it that he did not want to get further entangled with the politicians in the coutry?

"Sit down."

"Yes boss, yes boss," he said and bowed again.

"For the time being, cut out all this boss-thing, please."

"Yes, boss. I mean, yes, sir. But you see, sir, you are the boss. I am the lowest, lowliest man on the totem-pole. And when the boss was a white man, I always addressed him and called him boss, even behind his back . . . "

"Siddown, man!"

"Lemme stand, sir." His voice was hoarse. Pebbles seemed to be in his throat, rubbing against his vocal chords. It was a voice you associated with a man who drank heavily.

"Would you like a drink?"

"Oh no, sir. Sir, I couldn' drink in your presence! Certainly I couldn' drink whilst I am on the job, sir!"

John Moore could smell his breath. Vagabond passed his hand across his mouth, as if he too had smelled his own breath, and was wiping it away. His unshaven face cried out. John Moore smiled. This was going to be a difficult interview.

"How is your work?"

"Well, sir, I does my best."

"Good."

"Yuh can't ask for a more harder worker. I comes in here prompt at eight o'clock every morning, and when I leaves in the evening at five, I leaves all my work for that day done. And let me tell you something else, sir. I do not congregate with them other fellows who play dominoes and cards when your back is turn. And I don't join-in with them when they come to me telling me that they doesn't like working for no colored man, meaning you, sir. But I says to them, I say, 'If the powers that be appoint Mr. Johnmoore in charge o' we, who am I not to obey him?' I says that to them, sir."

"Tell me something. Do you know anything about the files missing from my office?"

Vagabond flinched, and said, "Do you mind if I sit down, sir? I got to sit down." He sat down. He took off his hat, which he wore as if it was part of his hair. Grey ran all through his hair. "Well, I going to tell you the truth, sir. As I always say, when a man tell the truth, he doesn' have nothing to be afeared of. Now, sir, I want you to lissen good to what I going say." He passed his hand over his face again. The whiskers cried out. "I have been in this job for fifteen years. Fifteen years this year, November coming. November the seventeenth is fifteen years I been in this job. And nine months, two weeks, four days and twelve hours, if you want me to be exact. I keeps everything up here." He touched his grey hair. "And never, sir, never in my born days have I ever been accused of larceny, or nothing so."

John Moore thought of all the documented complaints by staff members about Vagabond taking home things that belonged to the office. His favorite petty pilfering was taking home rolls of toilet paper and paper napkins. John Moore also thought of Kwame. The woman had said that Kwame talked too much. Now, who was he to believe?

"There are files missing from this office, and I want to know if you know anything about them. You clean this office even before I am here, on mornings ... "

"Tell me, sir, any o' them four missing files ... "

"How many files you said are missing?"

" ... what I was asking you, sir, is iffing any of them four missing files is the one with my personal file in it, because as you know, I is the lowest man in the totem-pole, and I have my pension to consider, so that is why I asked you ... "

"Who told you there are four files missing?"

"Nobody didn' tell me so, sir. I just figured that nobody would come in here, open a door that locked, and walk-out with only *one* file. Because, after all, sir, hardly anything would be contain in one file, so the person must have take two, or three, or four, or even five ... I just mentioned four out o' my head."

John Moore tried to trick him, and said, "As a matter of fact, there is only one file missing."

"Only one, sir? I thought they was four ... "

He closed the door behind Vagabond, and sat down, tired and confused, trying to understand what was really going on around him. Later that day he interviewed another employee, who turned out to be hostile. The man came in. He remained standing. He was cold. He was tidily dressed. And he did not smile. He knew he was handsome. And he knew he was smart. What should be the tactic with this man, whom John Moore never liked, but could do nothing about because he was also an efficient member of the staff? He decided to be straightforward with him.

"Did you, sometime this weekend just ended, or at any other time, come into this office without permission, and remove anything, anything at all from this office?"

"Wait! You calling me a thief? Are you accusing me of breaking and entering, 'cause if so, I would have to talk to my lawyers . . . "

"I'm sorry. That is all."

He could not understand why most of his staff was so insubordinate towards him; perhaps they all believed, like Vagabond, that a white master was better for them.

The cabinets with all the old reports, written by Englishmen, experts the government had brought into the country, and mostly on such subjects as "Culture In a Developing Society," "The Development Component of Native Cultures," and "Culture: Its Place in Government," also contained a bottle of scotch. He poured himself a large shot, a thing he had never done before. He took the drink without ice or water. And he drank it off in one gulp.

His private secretary came in with a handful of mail and some letters for his signature. There were ten letters to be signed. He looked at the dates on which they had been given to her for typing, and they were all more than seven days old.

"What kind of a secretary are you?" he asked her.

"But, sir," she said, in a soft voice, very brittle, water already settling in her eyes, "You give me too much work. And I have to take my daughter to piano lessons four times a week, and when the previous director was here, he used to give me time off to take my daughter. And he never had more than two letters a week for me to type."

She was not usually so long-winded. Something new, and strong, like resentment, had crept into her manner. There was hate in her eyes. He was becoming alarmed.

She started to write in her stenographer's pad.

"Now what are you doing?"

She continued writing.

"I am writing-down what you are saying to me. The union steward told me to do it," she said. She looked at him with hostility between her tears, her widow's body tight, and shapely; and he thought he saw her breasts move just a little . . .

He was glad, some time after, when she showed Juliet into his office. Juliet looked shabby; and he was not wearing those brightly colored custom-made shirts any more. He was like a man who sleeps in his clothes. His white beard was no longer trimmed and greased. And his hair needed a combing. John Moore poured two drinks of scotch and water. Juliet sat bolt-upright as he sipped his drink. He did not run his fingers under his moustache punctiliously, as he had on the previous visit. His manner was a bit more personable too. John Moore watched him, and noticed this casualness in his manner; a manner which said consolation more than anything else.

"There's a feeling in the air, old boy," he said, "that you're going to be leaving soon."

John Moore sipped his drink, and watched him carefully over the rim of the cheap glass. This man sitting before him was on a different quest from the first time, when he had been seeking a job.

"This files-business is just the beginning," he went on. "I don't want to be prying, but have you found out who took those files, yet?" He waxed his moustache with the water that came from the perspiring glass in his right hand. "I have been hearing that those files contain some very serious business, old man. It is said that some chap on your staff has a direct line to the Prime Minister, so you ought to be careful."

John Moore took him off that subject, and inquired about his job applications. He hadn't had any luck; and he doubted that he would, "unless there was a change," he said. He didn't say what kind of change he had in mind. But everybody in the country was talking about a change in government, and this could have been what was on Julie's mind. "You learn how to wait when you reach my age, old boy." And without preparation he said, "Terrible thing happened to old Weekesie, don't you think? Poisoned, you know. Poisoned." He held his glass up to the light, as if he was looking inside it to see whether there was anything there against which he ought to have been warned. Then he said, "Damn nasty business, this poison-business, you know. Poisoned because of photographs, they say."

They sat and talked about other things, and when Juliet had finished nursing his drink, he got up and said, "Well, old chap, just thought I would pop-in-and-put-you on your guard. Thanks for the refreshments." And then he left.

While he was sorting out the events of the day in his mind, John Moore looked up to see that the second staff member he had interviewed was standing in the doorway. The man came in, and as usual remained standing.

"I want to make a deal with you," he said.

"Well?"

"Your car. Your car have the same tires as mine, because my car is the same model car as yours, right? I want you, before you leave, to put your car-tires on my car. And I will put mine on yours. Mine are old. And anyway, you won't need them seeing that you're leaving soon . . . "

"Who told you I'm leaving? Leaving where?"

"The job, this job as director. It's all over the place, and I thought I would be the first to make this deal . . . there's a lotta other fellas on staff who make deals. At any rate, think about it. You want to know who got those files . . . "

John Moore thought it was time to leave the office for the day. He was going to drive himself today, in the rented car put at his disposal since his own was still in the garage.

In the car park he saw all the large, late-model cars that belonged to his staff, shining and well-cared-for. He went to his car and unlocked the door on the passenger side. He had been warned by the woman to keep the car doors locked at all times. When he forgot to do this he would rush out, in the middle of a meeting sometimes, and lock the doors. He put his briefcase on the seat and walked around to the driver's side. Sometimes, too, he would get in on the wrong side, accustomed to twenty years of having the steering wheel on the left. He would laugh at himself when this happened. Now, he unlocked the door on the right side; and as he was about to get in, his pen dropped out of his pocket. He bent down to pick it up, and by chance inspected the tire.

There was a matchstick stuck into the valve. His confusion gathered around him. He felt terribly alone. It was the same feeling he had had when he spent the night outside on the patio.

He inspected the other three tires, and there were three matchsticks in each of them.

He took his briefcase out, locked the door again, and went back into his office.

"What is wrong, sir?" said the man who had earlier bargained for the tires. It was the first time he had addressed John Moore as "sir." "Something is wrong with your tires?"

Without answering, he went back into his office, closed the door behind him, and called for a taxi. While he waited for the taxi to come, Kwame called on the telephone.

"I *have* to see you tonight!" he said, the breath going out of his voice.

The follow-up meeting promised by the *hoonta* was called for ten o'clock that night at the same house on the beach. The Minister called the moment John Moore reached home. "Hi, fellow! Your-humble-servant here!" John Moore could never detect from the Minister's voice and manner of speaking the seriousness of the matter he happened to be discussing; his voice was always so casual, with the intonation of a blues song. "Since your car is out of order," he went on, and John Moore became more wary, searching between each pause and inside each nuance for the real meaning behind the Minister's words. "I have a job for you, son. *Top priority. I* want you to jot down a few lines on this American destabilization that's being talked all over the country. You got me? *American destabilization.* Boy, I wish these blasted Yankees would behave themselves. Like the Canadians. I will get it cleared so that you can publish it and put it on television and the radio. Trust in Your-humble-servant, son. This is top priority. Make it a tough one, son. A tough one." When John Moore recovered from the shock of this latest request, and was listening more attentively, the Minister was saying, " . . . we have to protect this country, and this government. No sweat at all, 'cause we have Hitler on our side! . . . Are you going to be home all night?" John Moore told him he was staying in all night to work on some poems. "Good," the Minister said. "Work on them po-ems, boy. Stay in all night, son, and work on them po-ems." And the phone rang off.

He could feel the gun resting on his thigh. He felt more comfortable. And then he felt badly about feeling comfortable because he was wearing a gun. He must remember, though, that when the assailant confronted him, he must shoot to kill. To kill. He must also remember to drag the assailant's body off his property, and leave him at the side of the road. What would he do if the neighbors saw him dragging a dead man? And suppose the body remained at the side of the road all that night, and the next day too? Suppose the garbage men didn't come round. Think of the flies!

The maid had left for the day. His dinner was left in the oven. She always left it there, "to keep warm," she said. He spoke to her about this, and told her he preferred to have his dinner left in the refrigerator. Nevertheless, she continued to leave his dinner in the oven.

Tonight, however, he had no appetite for food. He would have a scotch. He was drinking "like a fish" these days. Nothing else seemed to settle his nerves. The telephone rang and he jumped.

"Hello? Mr. Johnmoore? This is the Southern Supermarket calling. Well, you see Mr. Johnmoore, your account with us . . . well, I was thinking . . . I was wondering when we're going to see you to settle-up the account? Now Mr. Johnmoore, we don't want to give you the wrong impression, that we are rushing you nor nothing so . . . we know you are a respectable gentleman, but we thought . . . "

"I'll send you a check in the morning."

"Well, you see, Mr. Johnmoore, a check normally would be alright, but seeing that there's all these rumors going round about you leaving . . . well, we wonder if we can't come in the morning ourselves, and collect the cash ourselves, Mr. Johnmoore . . . "

He went into the master bedroom and changed. He was too tired, too listless to have a shower. Instead he sprayed his underarms and between his thighs with deodorant, the gun resting on the counter beside the washbasin. He got dressed and walked back into the bathroom, and looked at his reflection. He was dressed in white. White African shirt, white linen trousers, white socks and white clogs. And he thought of a strange thing: when you are being prepared for the coffin in this country, you are usually dressed in white, from the inside out. *"One thing I want you to always remember, son,"* she had told him many years ago, *"is always make sure you have-on clean underwears. You could never tell when sickness will strike you, and you have to take-off your clothes in front of a doctor. Accidents will happen,"* His mother, that great woman of philosophy, was far from him now. And yet she was always in his thoughts. He was alone in another way. No family in the country with him. No roots. The bushes and the chalice vines on the roof of the patio outside were drying up. Their roots were defective.

He poured himself a scotch. It was his fourth already. He had no music here, no books; and the country seemed to sell only one magazine, *Time*, which he had given up reading.

The telephone rang again. He put down the scotch to answer it.

"Hello?" And for a long time, all he could hear was heavy breathing. "Hello?" He thought only women received these calls. He tried not to give the impression that he was frightened. "Hello?" Still no answer. So he put down the telephone. Immediately, he was sorry he had not held it longer. He realized that someone was checking to see if he was at home. At least two persons wanted him to be home tonight . . . *"And another thing I want you always to remember and never to forget, and it is this. When you come home at night or during the day, wherever you happen to be living, always look under your bed. And in every single cupboard and clothes closet or hole, where you think a man could hide himself. Don't you ever forget that, son."* She had told him this the same night that the man who lived in the house three doors from theirs was blown through the ceiling. The man had come home from work, and had collapsed tired in his bed. The bed had exploded; and the man went up into the sky with the bed.

He picked up his scotch, and it tasted delicious. He decided to take his mother's words seriously, and went through each room in the house, searching the cupboards and clothes closets and other places; and he even looked under the beds, although he felt foolish doing it. When he bent down to search under the bed in the master bedroom, he saw a penny on the floor in the dust. The maid was not so efficient as she thought. He must remember to speak to her tomorrow. As he stood back up, he could feel the gun pinching his thigh. It was a secure pinch.

Perhaps he was thinking too much; thinking too many evil things of these people. They were simple, upright people who went to church almost every Sunday. There were politicians and people living in the country: he must always remember this distinction. Perhaps he should go to the meeting. It would be the only way he could find out what was going on in the country; and what was being planned against him. He was a poet. He would remain a poet. Time, he felt, would turn the slander and the gossip against him into truth. The telephone rang. And he picked it up confidently this time, and said, "Hello!"

"*Don't move! Don't move from there! I coming up the hill!*"

It was the woman.

He had poured yet another scotch when a car drove hurriedly into the carport. He did not think she could get there so fast. But he relaxed. She was a remarkable woman.

He heard footsteps coming towards the front door. Could she have reached here so soon? He put his hand on the gun.

There was a knocking on the door. The knocking went on and on. And then he realized that the woman never knocked that way. His head was clearing from the drink. He waited. The knocking continued. The telephone rang again, and when he took it up, the woman said, "I'm leaving now," and hung up. He went to the door.

John Moore did not recognize the man. But he felt safe. He had his gun. And the woman was coming. So he invited the man inside. The man passed between him and the doorpost; and he had to move back to allow him to pass. The man walked straight to a chair and sat down. John Moore left the front door open.

"Can I use your bathroom?" the man asked, suddenly standing up. Johnmoore pointed down the hall. There were two bathrooms. The man went into the master bedroom, then came back and sat in the same chair, and looked around the room. John Moore sat and watched him. The man held one hand in the pocket of his shirt-jack.

"Well, I am here," the man said. And he made himself comfortable in the chair. John Moore watched him closely: all he had to do was keep him there until the woman arrived. The woman would be the witness. He needed a witness. The gun was rubbing against his thigh. He was watching the man carefully; and he thought he recognized him now, had seen him before, perhaps often; but he couldn't place the face in this present moment of tension and fear with violence on its breath. The man had a nervous habit of pushing his hand farther down into his pocket . . . he had seen this before . . .

"Well, I've come," the man said, shifting his position slightly in the chair.

John Moore's thoughts were racing: the Minister had asked him to remain at home that night; and now there was the caller who didn't speak. Was this the man they had sent to get him? Juliet had mentioned something about that too. So he sat and watched him closely, every move he made. And then relief came. The woman's footsteps came to the front door. They stopped. And the doorknob rattled, and she said, "Me! Open, Johnmoore!"

Courage and bravery and a violent passion surged into his body, and he got up and opened the door.

"Jesus Christ, Badger? Boy, what you doing all the way up here? You should be selling salt fish . . . "

"Good night, Mistress. I came and tell Mr. Johnmoore I come for the thing, but I can't understand. He put me to siddown, and two times now I tell him I come for the thing, but he ain' do nothing. I can't understand, Mistress . . . "

It was the cashier from Southern Supermarket.

"Johnmoore, why you keep Badger sitting down so, and won't even offer him a drink? You want a drink, Badger?"

Badger accepted. "Mistress, I was here sitting down, waiting to hear if Mr. Johnmoore was going to offer me one. But he like he didn' recognize who I is, and he didn' offer me one."

Johnmoore got up to get the cash for Badger. In the bedroom, he overheard Badger saying to the woman, "But Mistress, something like it wrong, yuh. Uh mean, I know you, and I know Mr. Johnmoore, but he had me frighten' as shite, yuh. I glad you come when you come, 'cause I was sitting down there in that chair nervous as shite . . . if you understand my language . . . "

"Never mind, Badger, never mind," he heard her telling the man. In the bedroom he was now without reference to any context of time and place. He wished the woman was in the bedroom with him, to drag him down into the red-white-and-blue clean sheets with the weight of her body. Or if he had the strength, for him to drag her down on the freshly laundered striped sheets, smelling of all the work the maid had put into them. He went back out and paid Badger. Badger smiled. It was the kind of smile which told John Moore that Badger was glad to get out of the house; perhaps, too, the smile was the anticipation of further smiles and some ridiculing laughter that would resound in the supermarket, when Badger told the people there that Mr. Johnmoore "like he going mad as shite, yuh!"

When they were alone, he and the woman, they sat facing each other, just as he had faced Badger and dared him to be violent. But this time it was like a crucifixion: he knew that if she had the courage to say it, she would tell him that he was losing a grip on himself; and he wondered why he had permitted himself to be so paranoid. But perhaps, he mused, neither of them should talk for the rest of the night.

"Do you still carry your gun?"

"I have it."

"That's what Badger said. He said he saw you touching it." She had reconciled herself to being with him, in whatever state he was in, now. "Make sure it's always loaded. Badger could have been somebody else."

"Would you excuse me?" he asked her. Inside the bathroom, he closed the door and took the gun out, trying to suppress the click of the ugly weapon; and he loaded it with six bullets. He had been walking around with the gun unloaded. *"Badger could have been somebody else."* He carried one shell in his pocket; and had been carrying it there for some time now. He had never loaded the gun, had never loaded a gun in his life. This country was changing him into a cowboy.

"You are so careless," she said, knowingly.

Was he going to become what they wanted him to become? Was this the price of his own survival? There was a saying in the country, "Brek for yourself!" He wondered how efficient he would prove in this regard.

"We have to protect you now," she said. "It's your turn now. But I hope it never comes, I hope it never comes ... "

No one, no circumstances before, had put the question, the possibility of his death, so bluntly.

"Did you check under the bed tonight?" And he burst out laughing.

"You should laugh more often."

It occurred to him that he should stop thinking about politicians and meetings and ministers; and should spend the rest of his time writing poetry. He wondered whether he would ever be able to write another poem while he remained in this country. Whether he would be able to write *the* poem about this country. Who were the other poets in the country? There were no poets in the country. Who were the painters in the country? There were no painters in the country. Who were the intellectuals in the country? The politicians. The politicians were the intellectuals in the country. He wondered whether he could ever say that aloud, in the presence of anyone.

"Did you hear that the director o' the culture-place say that there ain't nobody in this whole country who have brains?"

"Yuh mean to tell me that he could come from all up in Canada and make a kiss-me-arse stupid statement like that? Wait, do he think that we is fools? Man, we have the highest literate rate in the world! The Prime Minister o' this place is a kiss-me-arse intellectual himself!"

"There is too much careless talk in this damn country, if you ask me."

The word of his statement, should he be foolish enough to make one, would spread and cover the whole country within twelve hours, just as the sun and the rain covered the land at the same dramatic time. And there would be no arguments pro or con. Matters of argument were not settled like that. They were settled by the violence of language. *"He says that as colonists we have no intellectuals,"* the disseminated word would say. And the simple retort of their language would be, *"Oh, he's a fucking idiot!"* And that would be the end of all rational argument.

The woman was talking. "I don't mean to be insensitive. I don't mean to criticize you. But you are just a witness. Nobody like they're interested in hearing what you have to say, in your own defense. You are just a witness without a defense, without a mouth. That press conference you gave some time ago, they didn't let you broadcast that. And you know, I myself even forgot about it. That's the way it is . . . you even forget to fight for your rights, sometimes . . . just a damn witness, just a damn witness." The house had become quiet. He could hear the dogs on the hill and an occasional car coming or going. It had become a quiet night, with the stillness of death.

He realized that she was no longer speaking and he looked at her, and saw that she was crying. She had been crying for a long time. She just sat there, with the tears falling into the glass of sherry she held in her hand, without restraint, as if she had wanted to cry for a long time. "Sometimes, I even cry for Julie, although we're not . . . " She sat without moving, without even a spasm from the tears, and the water just fell down her face and appeared again on her close-fitting blouse, and on the table with the crystal glass. "We are just damn witnesses, me and you and Julie, just a damn witness." She searched in her handbag for a handkerchief, and when she was finished with it, her checks were like roses and her eyes were red. She blew some of the tears into her handkerchief, folded it neatly in its original fold, and put it back into her handbag. He remained silent and confused, useless to do anything about the crying or the events which were surrounding him. For a long time they looked at each other. He was resenting her strength and at the same time hating her for having broken down; and for having capsized such love at his feet, when he knew he was incapable of being responsible in the face of such passion and such love. And perhaps she was now, more than at any other time before, wondering whether he was really so weak as he must have seemed before her. But they were just two ordinary persons. They had been rendered harmful to each other in a most powerless way. Harmful to themselves, and to their mutual love; and powerless to do anything about it. Defeat seemed to come from both of them. He could feel the defeat. It was like an ague coming through his body, weakening him, making him forget the purpose in his life which was the poems he had promised to write. He forgot that the two pages of unfinished poems, two poems really, had been neglected in all this time. And he felt that he was unhinged from time, that time had come and he was useless to put it to its proper use and purpose. That all he was doing in this country was living. Not living it up; but simply living, since he was not dead. Perhaps, for all he knew, he was already dead. He could be dead, could be a dead man, as he sat looking at her. And she could indeed be dead too. His mother came back into his thoughts; far away from this her country too, a country which had proscribed her place and time many years ago; but she had left it, and had settled in a foreign land, and had never looked back. *"They don't owe you one blasted thing," she had said, recently, during a long-distance telephone conversation. "You just happened to be borned there, that's all. That's all. Get out. Get out fast, as fast as you can. I got out when I could. The only thing that that blasted place gave me is six children. America give me two apartment buildings . . . Brother-man! Brother-man, Brother-man!"*

"Brother-man? Brother-man?" The voice was mixed into reminiscences; he did not accept it and he faded it into the recollections of his mother's voice. But soon it was more pronounced and in the present, coming through the louvers, near where he was sitting with the woman. "Brotherman? Moorey?" She heard the voice by this time, separate from the feeling in the room with them.

"Don't answer," she whispered to him, and immediately made a sign for his gun. He felt his thigh and the gun was there. He looked through the louvers. Kwame was standing under the window, in the shadows, away from the outside lights that protected the house from intruders. John Moore said he would open the door.

"No need for that, Brother-man. I bring something for you. I didn't want to cause no disturbance in this neighborhood, so I turned off the motor just round the corner, and I walked here. I gone now."

John Moore took the parcel wrapped in brown paper, the kind used for groceries. He closed the louvers as the grassroots politician moved away. A cassette tape was in the bag, which smelled of fried fish.

"A tape," she said.

"A tape," he said, becoming more neutral than he liked himself to be. But he was feeling the same way she probably was: lifeless. Too much had happened now for alarm. It was as if they were both waiting for something dramatic, something deadly, something violent, to happen to both of them.

"There's a lotta nastiness on that tape, I bet you!"

"Dangerous."

"That too."

"Now, if anybody was to know that you and me were sitting down here, all night, not minding anybody's business, and all of a sudden you find yourself with this tape . . . would they believe it? That's what I mean by a witness. You see what I mean now? You are a witness. And I am a witness."

He had no answer for this.

"It's a tape of something," she said.

"Could be anything."

"Could be."

"Could be nothing at all on that tape."

"Could be."

He looked at the tape in just the same way as they were talking about it. He put the tape on the machine, and was about to play it when she said, "Don't play it!"

She held her hand on his. "Not now, please. Let's go in the bedroom." And she held out her hand to him, and he took it, and got up, and went into the bedroom with her.

The air inside the bedroom was cool although the louvers had been closed. It felt safer in there. She turned the table lamps off, and in the slight light from the bathroom door, which was almost closed, he could see her beautiful thighs as she began undressing. The surgeon's slice on her body was there. Her face was turned towards the wall. And he had the full unhindered view of her full strong body . . .

The sea rough as hell tonight! Like a woman!

— For a man of the cloth, your language is . . .

— Man, Mr. Chairman, I am not in church now. Render unto Ceasar . . .

— The sea pretty, though.

— Tell me Rev, who you say that Canadian woman is, maybe you could fix me up, eh?

— Mr. Chairman, you's a fucking old man, no pun intended. One o' these days you're going to kill your-blasted-self.

— Gentlemen, gentlemen, it's getting late and we have a lot of business.

— Okay, fellows. Meeting come to order!

— My colleague will be the chairman again.

— Okay, fellows. We successfully started the rumor to get rid of Johnmoore. All o' you know what's been happening. He won't be here tonight. As you know, something's to happen to him. Understand?

— Hick-hick!

— That's the way it has to be. That is pragmatism. All o' you have been briefed. We got the files from Johnmoore's office, and we planted them in the Prime Minister's office. With a little doctoring, of course. They were doctored-up before they reached the Prime Minister's office.

— Pardon me, but I think that was a master stroke! At last we got rid o' that radical.

— Albatross, eh?

— As soon as the people start gathering at the meeting that the grass-roots man here will be holding, we have a few fellows, about twenty men, who will go through the crowd and rough-up the people a little. Not too much. A few bottles going start pelting, and I have Hitler and the police on the

standby, ready to crack a few heads. Now the precautions are that Hitler and his boys will not touch Kwame, while he's on the flatform. Kwame will disappear when the fighting starts. A police car will pick him up, and take him to safety. Now, a word about the police. Men will be in plain clothes. We've decided not to have the police too conspicuous. Law and order, you see.

— If I may ask, when will the police know when to move in?

— I already discussed that with Kwame. He knows the code-word to use. And I know the code-word.

— He know and you know. Anybody else here know those codewords?

— If I may be frank, I don't think that everybody in a conspiracy needs to know every detail of the conspiracy. We are a hoonta. Bound in this common end. We know what the ends are. Tonight we discussing pure ends. Just the ends.

— Thanks, Rev.

— Number one. Loudspeaking equipment ready, organized and hidden. Naturally, we had to get it from the national culture office. They have the best and the loudest. We got it through the assistant director who, as you know, isn't exactly enamored that Johnmoore got the job as director. The equipment is signed out in the name o' the director, if you get what I mean.

— Hick-hick!

— Another master stroke, eh, Chairman? I don't have to remind you that we are dealing with danger. Possibly death. Political death included. Now, the Lord Bishop here . . . that's what he wants to be, that's what he's going to be! . . . Bish here will preach the sermon we decided on. And remember, Your Lordship, come down hard, damn hard on the idea of political dishonesty, political manipulation and American destabilization and involvement. The Church have power. So use it. The Church is the most powerful institution in the country. And mention how the Canadians are giving money to the Other

*party. The ends justify the means. The ends are, gentlemen,
that we are in a position to take-over this country. If violence is
the only answer, we will still be taking over. This is war. My
whole political future is at stake. And not even my mother is
going to screw-up this plan. The action is the ends. We control
the means of reaching those ends. And if the present Prime
Minister is still the prime minister the morning after, well
everybody's arse is going to be hot! Hot-hot-hot! So, you see
what I mean. The Reverend Bishop here . . . never mind me
calling you by your future title already . . . you gotta get used
to power, boy. So, Bish, you had better start walking-'bout with
with your iron underneath your cassock, heh-heh-heh!
Particularly on the night in question. Prevention is better than
cure, boy! Listen to Your-humble-servant. Now, we have the
guns hidden-away in three locations. On the night in question,
those locations will be known by me and one other person.
Now, let me tell you the purpose of all this violence. But before
I get to that. Kwame, the grass-roots man, is the key to every-
damn-thing that is to happen. I want him and everyone o' you
to understand that. Kwame is the key, if he can attract a big-
enough crowd . . .*

    — You saying I can't draw two thousand people?

    *— Wait, fellow. We know you held six last week,
wasn't it?*

    *— Seven. Seven in five nights! Not even the govern-
ment can draw the crowds I draw.*

    *— Mr. Chairman, I don't see why we are quarreling at
a time like this.*

    *— You could afford to talk shite! You are going to be
the Lord Bishop. You got that berry already without liffing a
straw. But what has this hoonta-thing decided to make me?
Eh? Everybody in here already forget the grass roots?*

    — Where do I come in, into the spoils?

    *— Oh hell, Chairman! I don't mean you Mr.
Chairman, I mean the Chairman. Chairman, you will be taken
care of. Everybody will be taken care of.*

— *Every-last-man-jack in this hoonta getting a berry!
Your-humble-servant give you his word.*

— *We have to be careful about leaks. Security is the
most important thing now. The same way we can get files
from people's offices, well, there's no need to go further . . . I
feel that somebody might even be trying to tape what we are
saying, right now. So far, thank God, our security is tight
enough that that contingency does not exist.*

— *And make sure that the Prime Minister is kept out
of this.*

— *That covered, fellow. Wait, you think we sleeping?
In the cabinet, we said a few things which made us know for
sure how the wind is blowing. And it's a' ill wind for somebody! But lemme remind you, we have to keep the lid on all
this, if not, there's going to be a lotta lashes sharing-'bout, a
lotta arses are going to be hotted-up, if any of this leak-out.*

— *What about the Americans?*

— *The Americans?*

— *Where the Americans stand in this?*

— *We have their backing. The ambassador is with us,
too. He had to. Uh mean, a fellow like him, come down here,
saying he is not backing a democratic movement of the people?
Wait, yuh want us to throw his arse back up in Brooklyn to
sell life insurance? This is the next government sitting down
right here, fellow! This is the next fucking government, take it
from me, Your-humble-god-damned-servant . . .*

— *And the Canadians? What about them?*

— *Those Candians think they're smart!*

— *The Canadian fellow with the beard, you know who
I mean, well, I will be meeting with him. As a matter of fact, I
am meeting him at the discotheque later tonight.*

— *But can we trust the Canadians, though? As you
know, the Canadians are always playing some kind o' waiting
game. They say their foreign policy isn't imperialistical.*

— *Isn't what? Where you been, fellow? As a minister,
I can tell you a few things about those Canadians.*

— *The Chinese?*

— *The Chinese not in this yet. For the time being.*

— *Hick-hick! Should I remind this hoonta that we are not planting rice. This is no agricultural revolution!*

— *Damn right!*

— *We have to deal with the Chinese nevertheless. Borned diplomats. And they been dealing with the Third World for years.*

— *The British? What about them?*

— *The who?*

— *British, nuh!*

— *What do you think we are plotting? To blow up Buckingham Palace? This is a developing country, fellow. The British are broke.*

— *Order, order! Now, we have to decide whether we are remaining in the Third World. Or if we are going with Cuba. That is to say, are we going to be hemispherical?*

— *That is external affairs you talking, isn't it?*

— *For the time being, I suggest we remain a Caribbean country. That way, we can qualify to get more loans from everybody, and some aid, and soft credit, as a developing poor nation.*

—*Concessions you are talking about, man. Concessions. What kind o' prime minister are you going to be? Haven' you read Fanon?*

— *Political pragamatism, boy!*

— *Blasted concessions, I say! Selling out the people, even before you is the fucking prime minister.*

— *Pragamatism, boy!*

— *Where does the Americans fit into all this, that is what I want to know. I need a' American visa to visit my daughter soon . . .*

— *Were you sleeping, Chairman?*

— *Where the Americans stand?*

— *We just said the Americans backing the hoonta.*

— *I must have been watching the sea. Good! I could*

get that visa, then. The sea getting rough . . .
— *The ambassador said so?*
— *From the horse's mouth!*
— *Hommuch money they putting in?*
— *One million . . .*
— *Jesus Christ! That is really America! The land of the free, and the dollar-bill!*
— *Local or foreign currency?*
— *Cold, Yankee-dollar-bills.*
— *As a matter of fact, I forgot as chairman of this meeting to tell you this. The money's here. My colleague and I have it already in a secret account, and I am pleased to say that . . .*
— *In who name? In whose name that money is?*
— *Well, listen, fellow. Whose name should we put it in? You don't trust your leaders? You don't trust Your-humble-servant?*
— *In who name that one million American dollar bills is? That is what I want to know.*
— *My name.*
— *And mine.*
— *That is all I want to know. And which bank?*
— *You don't trust me, boy?*
— *Which bank it in?*
— *The new one in town. The big one.*
— *Which new one?*
— *First National Mercantile Bank!*
— *That is all I want to know.*
— *Order, order! Order! Now, this is the part I left for the last . . . There're certain people that we have to get rid of. No need to say anything more. In every coup, certain people must be got rid of. Must be shot. Simple as that. Here then is the list. Pass it around. And who you feel like adding . . .*
— *Jesus God!*
— *The bishop too?*
— *Hick-hick! He wasn' born here, remember?*

— Well, fellow, how many bishops can we have in one small developing country? And how would Rev become bishop? You can't have your cake and eat it too.

— Hick-hick! Oh!

— I see we going be needing a new man at the Central Bank. Wonder if the hoonta would consider my brother-in-law who just graduated.

— Hick-hick!

— Jesus Christ!

— You see what I see? He gone through the eddoes, at last.

— You didn't think so, did yuh? We giving trade and commerce to the grass-roots man, here.

— Who getting the High Commission up in Canada? I see that we needing a man there. Perhaps the Chairman . . . they got a lotta young women up there. And the job never required no big lotta brains, neither. The last one didn't have none at all!

— Have you anyone to add to this list? You have until in the morning.

— I satisfied.

— Me too.

— Although I'm going to tell you something, now. I can personally think of a lotta fellows I could add-on 'pon that list, but I don't want to appear vindictive. This isn't a witch hunt. And we don't want to divide the country. Isn't there two more permanent secretaries we could add-on 'pon this list? Just to balance things . . .

— Man, that is a new-brand cabinet you got there, man!

— You think this is a picnic? And if things go according to plan, and we have to have elections, we holding the elections under the state o' national emergency. And after the elections, you going see something. Every man crossing over the aisle of the House, if we lost. And the same conclusion obtained. The ends, boy! The ends justify the means. Yuh

think *Your-humble-servant* in this for fun? It is a prime min-
istership at stake, fellow . . .

— Nobody mentioned anything 'bout the governor
general. What happening to the governor general?

— The governor general ain't dead yet. At any rate, he
don't trouble nobody.

— One thing I am glad for! This new government that
we just formed won't be running-offa pussy, like the last one!

"Have your gun?"

He felt his thigh, and the cold ugly metal thing was there. She revved up the car, and reversed it out of the carport.

It was a bright afternoon. He was slightly disoriented. It was the first time he had come outside for the day.

The car pulled around the corner from the house. Everything looked normal. So normal that he wondered whether he had actually listened to the tape. There was no comparison between that time of night and this time of sunlight. The land that ran down towards the sea was beautiful, as it had been entrancing each day that he drove along this street.

The car turned left and soon they were traveling along roads almost hidden by the tall uncut vegetation of cushcush grass and sugar canes that were ripe for the factory and the sugar and the sugar-cakes and the year-end bonuses. And before all this prearranged organization, there would be a few strikes by the sugar workers, and more hectic talking and bargaining by union bosses. He watched the sugar canes and felt that they could, in a natural manner, stand there for so many months in the hot savage sun, growing on their own, natural and majestic, and then all of a sudden have their sovereignty abused by the union bosses, who were men with not much social and agricultural education, and less human feeling. Somebody was being fooled, he thought, into believing that the union bosses had anything to do with the democracy of the sugar canes. The canes were the only beautiful things growing in the country; and yet all of a sudden, through a short-term exposure to socialism, the union bosses would inflict their half-understood necessity upon the beautiful harmless canes. The cane-fields were now raging and blowing in their molested sadness. Perhaps, someday, the canes would become mad and grow and grow and stifle all the union bosses; and strangle them out of space and dignity. Or the sugar canes would become so strong and tough that they would refuse to have their bodies emaciated by the cane bills.

They were approaching that same valley into which, months ago, it seemed years now, the arriving airplane had punched itself like a penis. The tourists on board had cheered. The pilot had brought them from one life to another one, without injury and without trauma. The tourists had cheered. And had called the land paradise. Where was the man who had wanted to know some cheap native women now? He wondered how many he had been able to get, at the two-for-one rate of exchange. If they met again, he wondered, on a similar journey, would they have a chance to exchange experiences? And would the tourist still call the country paradise?

"Would you mind the radio?" she asked.

The national number-one tune, "The Rate of Exchange," came on. She hummed along with the calypsonian. He thought of the portion of the tape which mentioned the junta's plans for the Central Bank. The calypso was only fun, "sport," as they said in the country. And the funny nature of the calypso was perhaps identical to the ridiculousness of the threat on the tape. He put the threat out of his mind, and concentrated on the pleasing tune. He did not even know the man who was in charge of the bank; and he did not know what his monetary and fiscal policies were. It was better to listen to the calypso. And enjoy the drive through the countryside, as he had seen the tourists do. He had taken the day off to enjoy the country. The land was beautiful. And he should get to know it again.

But he started to think about death. Here he was, traveling with the woman in her car; and the car could conceivably, in terms of averages, get into an accident. And if it were a serious one, he might be trapped within the metal on these lonely roads. And how long would it take for someone to come to their rescue? Or he might be thrown onto the road, and one of the fast-driving cars coming round the bend, with no speed limit, would run over him and finish him. And who would come to his funeral? He had no family and no relatives in the country . . .

"Was I talking in my sleep?" she said. "I had a dream last night that, as the old people would say, 'ride me, and ride me' like hell!" Every time a car came toward her, she would stop talking; and he would have to stop thinking. And then one car came around the corner. She saw the car just when it was right on her. She applied her brakes. He closed his eyes to shut out the noise of the collision. And when he opened them, the car was still swerving to get back on the correct side of the median.

"Jesus Christ!"

The young people in the car were shouting and laughing and singing "The Rate of Exchange."

"I was sitting down in a house," she was saying, when she had recovered, some way down the road. "In my sleep I was in this house that looked like yours, and in a way, like mine; and there was all this loud music like at the discotheque; noise and noise and lights flashing all over the place, and a man came in, and started to feel-me-up, and I thought it was you, so at first I didn't put up a fight; but then when he came closer I could smell him and his smell wasn't yours, and that's how I knew it wasn't you. And this man was sweating like the devil,

devil, and then suddenly all the noise from the music, and the lights, changed into glass, broken glass, and the discotheque started to break up, you know, like the sound of glass breaking . . . "

He tried to see, as most people would, whether his own interpretation of her dream could fit into the experiences of yesterday; or perhaps even if the dream was meant to relate to something about to happen today; for in his mind there was great foreboding. This always seemed the way with dreams. You might be living your own dream as you breathed.

"And that face won't come back to me!"

The car was climbing a hill. At the same time, a jumbo jet was coming in to land. He thought again of the tourist who had arrived with him; and of the new ones coming in now, to taste the paradise in the country and the women, and in some cases the men.

The radio announcer said that in five minutes the news would be on. Five o'clock. Time in this country either went quickly, before you could tell it had come and gone, or else very slowly, like a prolonged manic depression.

They were now on top of a very high hill, a mountain it seemed. And below them, in the haze of distance and colors untrue to the eye, was all the expanse of the country. There was no one in sight around them. There were cows lying down, and some standing, with bended heads, moving about the land, searching for the low stubble of grass which looked blue in the distance. On the left was the sea, everlasting as the sugar canes, not going anywhere, unchanging, except that the white running caps of water made it seem as if the whole sea was rushing ashore, just as the fishermen would come back home after a hard day in the waves. They parked the car, and watched.

"This country! It's the most beautiful in the world!" she said. But people always said that about their country. "The most beautiful in the world. Pity that the politicians don't always remember that!"

He was going to ask her the name of the hill they were on, but that would be to label his sightseeing, just as visitors have to do, in order to tell stories back home. He was not a visitor. Standing on this hill, he promised himself that he would remain; would remain, and fight . . . and fight to remain. For him, it was enough that he was here, this afternoon, privileged to be seeing this part of his country he had not seen before. He was going to remain.

"I wonder how it was when the first man came here," she said. "Not a person in sight. Not a care in the world. It must have been paradise!"

The news was coming on. She raised the volume and settled back, with her head against the leather, her eyes closed. The peace of the mountain-hill and the breeze of that cool altitude, and the impossible reliving of the hill's first experience, relaxed her face. She was smiling. Just as she smiled after making love. Particularly if she was satisfied, and had time to doze and dream of "the sweetness," as she called it, in her body.

Quite suddenly, he was sitting upright at the announcer's voice: " . . . *that a bomb exploded in the office of the Director of National Culture. Police said it was the worst explosion in the country's history. The director, Mr. John Moore, who recently took up the post, was not in his office at the time of the explosion. Police and reporters have been trying to locate Mr. Moore all day. The estimated damage to the director's office is five thousand dollars. Damage is complete, and the chair in which the director sat was a mangled wreck. Police have not ruled out sabotage as the cause of the bomb explosion . . . Stay tuned to this station for more details . In the meantime, we repeat the headline of this news bulletin . . . "*

On their way home, the same news was repeated. They got out of the car, and locked it. They locked all the doors, and turned on the television. The radio was on too. But the house was quiet.

"Let me check through this place, just in case," she said.

"How many days, exactly, are there before Easter?"

"Why?"

"Easter."

"One day!" she shouted from the bedroom where she was inspecting.

He was puzzled. Something must have been changed. He was no longer a witness, as she called him. He was involved. Something must have gone wrong. He was going to find out.

"You have your gun?" He did not bother to answer her. In the bedroom, she was banging doors and drawers. He rested his hand on his thigh, and it was there, cold and like a dead snake. He turned the radio up, just in case. There was another interruption of the musical program to bring listeners up to date on the explosion. A few details were added: the Prime Minister had made a tour of the director's office, accompanied by the chief of national security. John Moore was waiting for that one statement which would explain why the plan had been changed. He would know it when he heard it.

"If the telephone rings . . ."

And just then, it rang. It rang and rang. If he had been alone, with the news already broadcast, he would have answered it.

"Don't!"

"That man Badger did a strange thing when he came here last night," he told her. "First thing he did was go to the bathroom. Of course, he asked me. But it seemed strange . . . "

"No, no, not Badger," she said. "He was more scared of you . . . "

"You think so?"

"He told me so."

The main evening news came on the radio.

"A dramatic turn in the events surrounding the bomb explosion in the offices of the newly appointed Director of National Culture was seen late this afternoon, when the Prime Minister held a hastily summoned cabinet meeting. The cabinet meeting is believed to have been called to discuss aspects of the bomb explosion. Sources close to the Prime Minister's office said that two ministers were absent from the emergency meeting. The ministers, whose names have not been released for security reasons, could not be reached at their respective ministries.

"The Prime Minister is believed to be preparing a statement for broadcast to the nation later this evening . . . "

He turned the radio off, and waited.

"Do you think they'll come?" She rested her hand on his lap. He rested his hand on his thigh. And to ease the waiting, she turned the radio back on. There was music on the radio. And it was a few minutes before the television news. He got up and opened all the louvers in the house. Dusk was falling. And he flung open the door leading to the carport. She sat watching him.

"You're exposing yourself, you know."

"I want to see them when they come. I want them to see me when they come."

"Let me get you a drink."

She got up and fixed the drink. He had eaten nothing all day. But he was not hungry. There was a

tightness in his guts. Only drink could settle it. She did
not make herself a drink. They would wait, together. He
was glad, after all, that he was not alone.

"I wonder what my mother is doing now?"

"I wonder what's the time?" she said.

" . . . *and gentlemen, we interrupt this program to
bring you the audio portion of a television press conference
now in progress, and being held by the minister of . . . *" She
turned up the volume of the radio and he turned down
the volume on the television. He wished the press conference was being shown on television.

The Minister's voice came on smooth and sure.

"Your-humble-servant," she said. But he had
already recognized the Minister through his manner of
speaking.

"*I have always been a member of the grass roots. Most
of you out there listening to me know my father and my mother. My father was a grass-roots man, too. A man from the
people. But never before in my political life have I condoned
violence. In any shape. In any form. In any manner. This
country which I have the humble honor to represent has the
reputation, and I may add, the best reputation in this entire
region, of being the most stable, most demo-cratic country. All
of us in government, and all of you, support our Prime
Minister. Our Prime Minister is one of the world's leading
statesmen. And I have always given him my fullhearted support. You-all know that. Imagine therefore, my personal con-
ster . . . concern, my personal concern, my personal shock,
when I learned earlier today that some persons in this community have sought to link my name and my ministry to a plan to
overthrow this honorable government!*" John Moore could
imagine him broadening his smile; and his eyes would
close, and look absolutely vicious, although he would be
smiling. His voice became more informal when he said,
"*I didn' mastermind no plot. Not Your-humble-servant! I
want to make it public now. That never in my thirty years of*

political life, serving the needs of the people of this country
have I ever done, have I ever said, have I ever felt, entertained,
have I ever instigated anthing, anything at all, or any action
that would serve to compromise my moral, political and philo-
sophical integrity. Good night, ladies and gentlemen. And
may God bless you."

"I hope they lock-he-up!" she said.

Soon afterwards the telephone rang. Before he
could remember her caution, he answered it.

"Mr. John Moore? This is GBS calling. Can we
get a statement from you on the violence that has erupt-
ed in the country since your return here?" He dropped
the receiver. She didn't even ask him who had called.

The telephone rang again.

"Mr. Moore? Well I so glad! Where was you all
afternoon, all day? I been worrying over you, all day, sir,
trying for the longest time to get through to you!" It was
his maid.

"Oh, I went for a drive."

"Thank God! You hear what going on in this
place?" Her breath was short. "Lord, Mr. Moore, they
fighting down here. I never seen a thing like this before
in this country. Not since the Riots, and that was before I
was borned. My mother had to tell me all about the
bloodshed and violence." He concluded that the people
had gathered in the city, according to the plan. He
would have to listen carefully. "And Mr. Moore? My
belly burned me when I hear the man in the radio say
that you nearly get blow-up in your office. Mr. Moore, I
hurted all over when I hear that. And now, look, I just
see a little child get shoot-down by the police. The police
like they gone mad. The police gone mad, Mr. Moore.
The police which uses to be such good protectors o' poor
people, now turning 'pon the same poor people.
Everybody gone mad, the shooting and the violence. But
are you all right, Mr. Moore? Did you see your dinner in

198 T H E P R I M E M I N I S T E R

the oven that I left to keep warm? When the man in the
radio said that you nearly get blow-up in your office, Mr.
Moore . . . " Her voice faltered here. " . . . and I hear
people saying that it would have serve you right to get
kill, because you come down here to start a revolution,
or something. But I tell them that isn't true, that's isn't
correct, darling. Not the Mr. Moore that I know!"

"Where're you now?"

"I here in my little house, Mr. Moore. And I not
crossing this door for no man! You might not even see
me in the morning, praise God. Saving this wickedness
stop by then."

He asked her where the fighting was.

"All over the place. All over the place. Appears
it started in the city, in the Market Square. But I hear
that it spreading like a cane fire now. It all over the
place. They say that two hundred already killed or
dead. Lots more injured and afflicted with wounds and
still more are deading, in the hospital. They say that the
hospital full-up with the wounded. It is like in the War-
days, Mr. Moore. But I say, these is the last days. The
last days. I read about these days in the Bible every
night before I go to sleep. Anyhow, I going see if I can
keep you inform, if this telephone don't cut-off in the
meantime. Take care of yourself, sir. And don't let *your
mother* come near your house. There is a cutlass in the
place where I changes into my uniform. You better run
out there and get that cutlass to protect yourself with.
Good night, sir."

"The maid," he said. "They're fighting in the city.
People have been shot."

"You think they'll come up here?"

He had never thought of that. He never thought
of a mass of men coming up into this exclusive district;
probably because the sociologists had claimed that the
country was arranged in such a way that an outbreak of

fighting or burning would stop at natural boundaries. But those boundaries did not bar the spread of burglaries. Perhaps this violence, which the sociologists did not believe in, could in fact spread all over the flat land, like an enraged cane fire. The maid had seen it right. It could be like a cane fire.

The telephone rang again.

This time it was the neighbor on the right, the expatriate. "What's going on, John? Are you people having a revolution in the country? They said on the radio that the PM has fired the entire cabinet. Have you heard this? Oh, incidentally, you were lucky as a bitch not to be sitting in your chair this afternoon. Christ!" The neighbor did not wait for comment, but put down his receiver before John Moore could say anything. Perhaps he just wanted to know that on his side, next door to him, someone was still alive.

The sound of rifle fire could be heard in the distance. How close were they? He wondered how they would come; and he thought he should close the louvers. But still he felt it would be better to be able to see them when they came. Looking out, he noticed that his was the only house that had lights on. The neighbor on the left, the retired American postal worker, was closed up in her safe house.

The streetlights were not burning. When he looked where he knew the sun went down every day, he could see almost the same color of light as the sun gave off when there were no clouds in the afternoon sky. It was the haze from the fires in the city. It looked as if the entire city was burning. But it might have been his imagination or his expectation. Kwame must have made an excellent speech! He wondered what had happened to him; what would happen to him? All that portion of the sky which signified the city in the distance was the color of thick smoke. He imagined the shouting and the screaming. And he tried to picture Hitler in all that smoke and screaming. Perhaps the people would be roaming through the exits of the city, on their way outward . . .

The most important clue to what he was hoping to hear would be the Prime Minister's statement later tonight.

"Make me a sherry, please," she said. "And it doesn't matter if it's sweet or dry." She smiled. And he knew that in the present circumstances she was prepared to forego her preference for sweet sherry. She smiled. But the beauty in her smile was not there.

Hours later, they were still sitting in front of the television, waiting for the Prime Minister's statement. "During the days of the War, in other countries," she said, "it must have been like this, eh? People sitting and waiting for sirens, and when they didn't come, perhaps out of habit the people still went on sitting . . . "

The streetlights were still not burning. News about the disturbances was in pieces. The skies below, down the hill, were bright. But it was far away still. The reflection of flames could be seen moving against the background of clouds which had gathered to block the moon. The moon was almost red.

The maid called again to tell him that taxi drivers were now in on the fighting and the looting. He thought of the taxi driver who had grown up with his father. The maid said some men had started pulling down the doors of shops and groceries and that they were running through the streets with their hands full of bottles of rum and cans of corned beef. No big department or clothing stores had been looted. People running by under her window had told her all these things, the maid said.

The woman loosened her belt, and slipped off her sandals. She unbuttoned all the buttons on her blouse and tried to relax. He watched her, and wondered how he would protect her when the time came. Would they have a chance? There was nowhere he could run to, nowhere she could hide him. There was no exit road from this exclusive development. That was what he had always hated about the street and the area. There was only one road to take. To walk on this street on a night like this . . . The telephone rang.

"It backfire, Brother-man!" It was Kwame. "It

backfire! They used me, Brother-man, so I going into hiding. I gotta run . . . "

The radio program was being interrupted for a news bulletin. *"The Minister . . . who declared his . . . for the government at his press conference was arrested at his home earlier this evening."* The radio was now like a bad connection of an overseas call. Something was being done to the power in the country. *"The press were not allowed . . . will keep you up to date . . . "*

"Your-humble-servant," she said. "I never liked the bastard!" He wondered what her reasons were for this hostility. "I am sorry for his family, though. And his wife."

But he worried more for Kwame. They would make sure that he bore all the blame. He would be forgotten soon, and perhaps, in another five years, there would be another grass-roots leader like Kwame whom the ministers and the politicians would coach and program to make their exploitation of the poor people more palatable. It would always be the same with the representatives of the grass roots.

The time came. The cameras showed the Prime Minister, sitting comfortably at a table on which was a letter basket, and behind him, on the right hand, the national flag in all its splendor. John Moore watched him closely, on this rare occasion of seeing him from the front, wiping heavy perspiration from his heavy-set face. These details were important to John Moore. The Prime Minister put his hands to his spectacles, looked seriously as if he was about to give some military command, as if he was about to give life sentence to all his ministers, and then he took the spectacles off again. He could sense the tension in the television studio. The Prime Minister breathed deeply inward, relaxed, and the perspiration poured down his face. He did not have time to use the large white handkerchief, now rolled like a wet piece of paper napkin. *"Good night!"* he said, like a military command. He paused for a while, as if he had forgotten what else he was going to say. *"Good night, ladies and gentleman. I come before you tonight in a time of crisis. National crisis. It is fit for me to come before you, because I am the legal . . . the constitutionally legal head of this country. And of this government. Let me tell you something about that constitutionality. This country is a free independent country. It has its due place in many international bodies, significant among which is the United Nations. This, and other reasons which I won't go into at this time, provides this country with full sovereignty. This sovereignty means that no other country, no matter how big or how small, how wealthy like the United States of America, or poor as the poorest developing African nation, no country can lawfully interfere into the internal affairs of this country. Certainly, I may add, not while I am Prime Minister. Ladies and gentle-*

given you this summary of the constitutional background of this country, so that what I have to tell you now will be clear, crystal clear.

"The security forces of this country have learned today . . . have learned today that a foreign government has been involved in the internal political situation now existing in this country. As a matter of fact, that government has financed certain subversive activities carried out by certain persons, known as the Junta. I will not call names now. But my government knows who that country is, and who those persons are. What I want to tell you tonight, ladies and gentlemen, is that firstly, the cabinet met earlier tonight in an emergency session. And secondly, that two ministers . . . two former ministers have been asked to resign. I am pleased to announce that I have accepted their resignations." Perspiration was oozing down his face. He took out the handkerchief and started to wipe it away; but realizing that he didn't look statesmanlike wiping his face on television before his country, he pushed the handerchief up his shirt sleeve. *"They have resigned. Thirdly, there have been disturbances in the city. I am informed that these disturbances have spread to other surrounding parts of the city. I am also informed that the lives of five hundred persons have been unfortunately taken in these disturbances. I want to assure all of you listening to me and watching me, tonight, that the police force, who have proven themselves again to be the upholders of the law, and of law and order in this country, have been able to put down the insurrection.*

Certain persons, members of this so-called Junta, have already been arrested. They are being interrogated by the police and the security forces.

"Ladies and gentlemen. In times of elections, when a country is preparing for a democratic general election, as this country is, will be in a short time . . . there is the tendency on the part of foreign representatives in the country to meddle in the internal affairs of a sovereign state. I want every one of

you listening to me and watching me on this television program to rest assured that I shall not tolerate the interference by any foreign government, or of any foreign government's ambassadors, in the peaceful running of this country.

"Some of the persons already arrested have confessed to having received monies and other incentives from a certain foreign government. We know this. We also know the amount of money invested by that foreign government. It is in the vicinity of six million dollars, foreign currency. Six million dollar-bills as the local jargon goes. I sometimes am at a loss to understand how certain so-called world powers arrange their priorities. That sum of money, six million, or twelve million dollar-bills local currency, which that foreign government saw fit to invest in the so-called Junta, for revolutionary purposes and intent against this country, to invest in the destabilization of a peaceable, of a peaceful democratic country, is precisely the amount of funds we asked for from an international monetary agency two months ago, to assist us in our development projects, among which is the high unemployment in this country. I am shocked at the priorities of those countries who profess a love and a pride in the freedoms of all mankind, and then turn around and promote dictatorships in this part of the world!

"Ladies and gentlemen. The disturbances which you have witnessed, some of you, in this country this evening, started quite simply as a bomb explosion in the offices of a government department. It was a stroke of luck that that officer was not at his desk, where he normally would be, doing the government's business, at the time of the explosion. But God moves in a mysterious way. And from that single explosion, with premeditation this so-called Junta sought further to implicate the director in their plot. This so-called Junta became the agents of a foreign government. They are misguided citizens. They planted foment and destruction throughout our capital city. The headquarters of government is in the city. Where the government functions daily, every day and some-

times late into the night, has had to be cordoned off by the police and the security forces. Other government offices of a sensitive nature have been cordoned off also, and are being guarded against sabotage.

"The atmosphere in this country for the past ten years, while I have been your Prime Minister, has been such that general elections, or even a by-election, could be held without fear or suspicion of tampering or undue influence by one political ideology or another. The political atmosphere has been such that elections could be held, and have been held, in a free democratic way . . . where the expression of all political feelings have been welcomed . . . including sometimes the strange theological philosophy of the Church.

"Ladies and gentlemen. As the head of the state, I am also commander-in-chief of its armed forces. I am in command of its security forces, also. I would be lacking in the collective responsibility which I obtained constitutionally and therefore legally, from you, if I did not do something to avert the disintegration of law and order in this country. I would indeed be remiss in my responsibility as the leader in this country, if I did not put an end to these foreign-aided political disturbances.

"I have therefore consulted with the Governor General, as I am bound by law to do. I have informed the Queen in Executive Council, Her Majesty Elizabeth the Second, as I am bound to do by my membership in Her Majesty's Privy Council. And I want to inform you now, ladies and gentlemen, of the actions I have taken, reluctantly. Reluctantly, because above all, and in spite of all, I believe in, and am an upholder of social democracy.

"I wish to inform you, ladies and gentlemen, of these actions.

"One. The cabinet as it existed this time last evening, is now disbanded.

"Two. The police, the armed forces, the security forces and the Coast Guard, are now the legal instruments of law and order in this country.

"*Three. Inasmuch as the political situation in the country, by virtue of the present large-scale disturbances, is unsafe to life and limb, and for the democratic system of government, and for elections to take place, I have advised the Governor General to issue an official proclamation canceling the published date of the general election. Elections will now be held, and will only be held, when the political climate is safe.*

"*Four. In view of the foregoing, and by the powers vested in me, as commander in chief, I have declared this country to be, from this moment and until further notice, in a state of national emergency. This emergency to have, while it lasts, the attendant aspects of a state of emergency.*

"*Five. I have declared this country a republic from this . . .* "

It had happened. This, he knew, was what he had been waiting for all evening.

"One thing I must say for that man," she said, "he is blasted smart!"

She had sat beside him throughout the speech, and not a word had she uttered. She seemed to understand it all, even before it was said.

It was by a stroke of luck, when she happened to look outside to see the morning breaking, that she saw instead the three men creeping toward the house with sticks in their hands. She did not recognize any of them. Silently and swiftly she led him through a window in the master bedroom; and just as silently, they ran down the hill in the direction of the sea. Moments afterwards they saw the flames, and could only guess what had happened . . .

People were everywhere, wandering about aimlessly, as though in a daze. None of them seemed to be fully aware of what had happened. Their lives, they knew, would go on just as before. It was the politicians, they said, and those who had been caught in the net, who would have to start running.

And many of those, the woman had told him, kept their Canadian landed immigrant papers up to date, or carried their Canadian passports on their persons, just in case the time came. And the time had come.

He wondered how many of them he would be meeting at the airport this morning. Those who had got away would be there. But from reports on the radio, not many had got away.

The large department stores in the city were closed. Only the small ones were open, as if in celebration of the new system which would help them to become large in time. The road to the airport was jammed with taxis. They were filled with tourists. "One thing about them," she said, "they're always the first to run." She had insisted upon driving him, "perhaps against my better judgment," to the airport.

"It's too hot now," she said, about the tourists, "for them to sun themselves!" She had talked about many things that last night, at her house. "That man smart as hell," was what she said most often. They had made love, in her four-poster, like a ritual, for the last time. They both knew it was a farewell. And before he dozed off, he thought he heard her saying, "That man is so smart . . . "

Some businessmen he recognized were on the road this morning. By all appearances they were going to the airport. He had met many of them at cocktail parties. But how many of them would be permitted to leave? Travel documents would be almost impossible to get so soon, so early in the morning. And this caused him to think of his own situation. For him, it had never been a question of permanency in the country anyway. He had always kept the return portion of his Air Canada ticket on him in his wallet. Folded and torn, but up to date and valid.

It was time to go. There would be nothing more for him in the country. It was different with the businessmen. They could always wait until the situation settled down to normal again. But for him, the situation would never get back to normal. It had not even been normal when he first arrived. There was widespread discontent; and everybody was critizing the government, though not too openly, saying that the Other party deserved a chance for change. But no one, not even the Minister and his colleagues, the Reverend Lionel Lipps and the Chairman, could have foreseen this turn of events.

"That man is a damn genius," she said. She would be saying this for a long time to come.

The airport was crowded when she parked the car. She had gotten a friend of hers in security to retrieve the car where she had parked it near his house when they had returned from seeing the country that day. She had gotten one of her contacts at the airport to arrange his reservation. Even in this, his final flight from his country, she was so consistently efficient, and invaluably well connected.

There were many people whom he recognized; but some of them turned their backs on him; and some, in feigned casualness, pretended that they were assisting with their friends' luggage. But this was no time for vindictiveness. He was leaving; and, he told the woman, he was leaving never to return.

"Don't say that," she had begged him, pressing her moist lips over his, to stifle any further declaration of what she called his "damn stupidness." "You born here, boy. Not even the Prime Minister could prevent you from coming back, if you want to come back. And I think you should come back . . . Not even *he*, even if he make himself President, or *Field Marshall*, could stop you. You born here!"

They were heading now for the boarding area. And she held him back to get the last sight of him. It was a morning so full of sadness.

Only the tourists seemed to be happy. For some of them, the radio said, had left their hotels without having settled their bills. A man in the line ahead said, "All these bloody poor-ass countries are the same! No god-damn good! They're all communists!"

And some men, taxicab drivers, gathered around the gate, arguing about the merits of a republic as against a democracy. And all of them said what a powerful and brilliant man the Prime Minister was.

"Not Prime Minister no more," one said. "President! Pres-i-dent!" he repeated, with some bravado for his knowledge of political systems. "And the minister that he lock-up, well he is the same one who uses to walk-'bout this place, saying he would make a more better prime minister. Well, be-Christ, by this time tomorrow morning, the Pres-i-dent will have his arse out in the hot sun, brekking-up rockstones!"

One more cautious taxicab driver said, "I did always suspect that something so was going to happen. And let me tell you why. People been walking-'bout this country for the last two or so months, saying we going loss the elections. Loss the elections? That man have never loss a fucking elections yet! Republic in your arse, now. That is how we going loss the elections. Republic in your arse!"

"I wonder, though, what he is going to give himself," an older one asked. John Moore recognized him.
He was the driver who had told him all about Pond.

"How you mean, give heself?"

"Like in the way o' titles," the man said. John
Moore wondered whether he should approach him and
say goodbye.

"Generalissi-fucking-mo!" The first, talkative
man said, with pride. "Generalissimo, in your arse!"

"A master stroke, though. Did yuh see him last
night, 'pon the telly? With water in his eyes, crying for
the nation? And bemoaning the vi'lence and the foreign-
er-people who send the vi'lence in dollar-bills? Didya
see the Chief, though?"

"What kiss-me-arse cry-water you talking about?
That was sweat, man! Sweat. Well, perspiration, then.
The man was sweating-through the thing like a gorilliphant!" He spat noisily beside where they were standing. "What you think it is at all, to run a country like
this? You think it is eating a sweet-bread? You think it is
a fucking sweetbread? Is sweat, man, *sweat.*"

"By the sweat o' thy brow," said the man who had
told John Moore about Pond. He saw him, and moved
away from the men, slealthily, to greet his friend's son.
Just as he was moving away, another man was saying,
"Lord, I can hear the calypso that Leadpipe going com-
pose 'pon this!"

The taxicab driver was now standing beside John
Moore. He put his hand on his shoulder, and said, "I
sorry yuh have to go. But it might be the best thing."
There was water in his eyes.

That beautiful black woman with the blessed body would be left with the country and those who wanted to rape it. He was heartbroken to have to leave her behind; but he felt it was only for a short time . . .

She told him to look in his pocket and he would find something. From her.

"Please. Don't take it out till you get on the plane."

He was standing holding her around her waist, but the number of people there made it uncomfortable for him to be more loving. He could feel her body so close to him at this wrong time; and too soon, far away from him. And he started to wonder. And thoughts of doubt and distrust came onto his brow in furrows and frowning.

"Don't worry about me," she said. She was always so thoughtful. They hadn't had time to permit their love, and their love for the country, to grow. It had been a forceful growth, their love: like a fruit, like a mango which had to be eaten while it was still ripening. "Force-ripe," the people called it. But it was a beautiful time of growing. Because like the land, and the sunsets which they had watched so many afternoons together on the beaches, the time had been ripe.

"Go. Just in case. I don't feel safe here at the airport. Go," she said, kissing him. Her lips were not wet this time. Only her eyes. And this alone made him go through the door. The officer there, who had nodded to him many times on previous occasions, when he went to meet dignitaries, looked at him this time, and did not know him.

"Yuh can't come back out through this door!" he said.

His voice was as sour as the feeling of this kind of departure.

As you leave, just as when you arrive, the land is the most beautiful thing about the country. There is the valley, shining and dripping wet with the formation of dew in its lap; and the small houses which really look as if dolls live in them. And the land from this vantage point is the closest thing to paradise that any human being can perceive. For none of us has really seen paradise. Paradise is in the mind; and when the mind is contented, a country such as this does look like paradise. Perhaps the tourists understand more about countries where they spend bought time and lots of money. Perhaps, too, it is the idea of flight, and departure that comes as a natural consequence of arrival, that makes the tourists regard only this aspect of a country.

"It was such a paradise!" a woman says, sadly.

"Not a bad place at all," the man sitting beside her says. "If only they had decent politicians. But politicians are the same the world over!"

It must be that. It must be the politicians who give the disposition by which a country is known; both to the country, like a returned gift, and to the citizens of the country.

The letter is in his pocket; he will read it later on. For the moment, there is still her presence. And the letter will be only a memory of her. He feels his thigh, checking his change purse, and the gun is there! There will be a problem about that at Toronto, at the airport. But there is time for that.

For the valley is rushing towards him now, and he must see it in its naked purity for the last time. And the land is beautiful, the only truly beautiful thing about this country.

First printing in 1977

ISBN 1-55096-066-0

9 781550 960662